"THE BEST METHODS ARE ALWAYS
TIMELESS, YET TIMEI

"TO WHAT EXTENT ARE OUR WANTS AND DESIRES SHAPED CONTEXTUALLY BY THE LIFESTYLES OF THOSE AROUND US, RATHER THAN BY ANY ABSOLUTE NEED?"

— Rory Sutherland

I love this quote, but it's not quite right.

Allow me to make one very minor adjustment ...

"TO WHAT EXTENT ARE OUR WANTS AND DESIRES SHAPED CONTEXTUALLY BY THE PERCEPTION OF THE LIFESTYLES OF THOSE AROUND US, RATHER THAN BY ANY ABSOLUTE NEED?"

Ahh, that's better.

Onward.

Here's to the forward-thinkers; the ones told that they cannot think for themselves. Here's to those destined for greatness, frustrated by the status quo. The ones who want to build a dream life. The ones who work to live; to love, and to smile.

Here's to those who don't just want to get by, but want to do something special with the short time that they have. The ones unwilling to trade their best years for "freedom" at 55.

The only people for me are the ones who are in this for the long run. They operate with integrity, passion, and with pride. They know that life is too short to spellcheck and they bring a book on the bus instead of shooting pigs with birds.

The only people for me are the ones who know that emotion trumps all else because people will forget what you did, but they will never forget how you made them feel.

Here's to those who know that focus leads to observation and observation leads to forward-thinking; that the next best thing is likely no better than that last best thing, it's just different.

Buttons change, humans don't.

Here's to those not interested in learning about every new gadget, widget, or whatsinit.

Facebook, Twitter, and Pinterest might not be around in five years, but humans will be. And that's why without a keen understanding of human needs, values, and desires nothing else matters. Because the only way to do something special in this crazy world is to first move backward by studying human behavior. Only then can you innovate.

Here's to those *they don't see coming*.

They wrote you off as being a crazy fool but you are getting better every single day. You know that the longer it takes for you to be noticed, the better you will be. And the World needs more crazy fools like you.

This book is dedicated to my Mom and Dad, as always.

Notes to the Reader

1. All stories are real, especially the stuff about me refusing to speak in Starbucks' made up language just to order a coffee.

2. Instead of cluttering up the text, I decided to omit references, scientific papers, and further reading sources from the published book. You can find all references and sources at: www.viralnomics.com viralnomics-references/

3. I use the term "the guy" a number of times throughout this book - it's gender neutral. I also use "he" and "she" interchangeably throughout the text.

4. A few sections are similar to ones from a previous book of mine called *The Race to the Top*. That book is no longer in print because, well, it wasn't very good. Some sections deserved to live on and are included in some form or another here.

5. Throughout this book there are jokes. Some are inside jokes between friends and others are obscure media references. If you find them, tweet me at @jon_ptdc and I might send you a prize. If you don't find them, take solace that you probably watched a lot less bad TV in the 1990's than I did.

I'll trade you a free copy of the audio version of this book for a picture of yourself holding it or an Amazon review. Go to www.viralnomics.com/free-audio" to claim your copy.

Viralnomics
"How to Get People to Want to Talk About You"

ISBN-13:
978-1518880971

ISBN-10:
1518880975

Jonathan Goodman

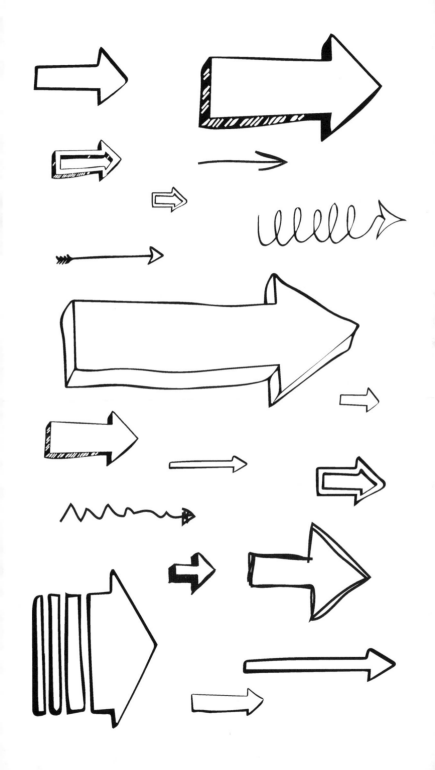

Our Story Begins in the 1870's

In a time when the horse and buggy was the primary mode of transportation, a British portrait photographer had a silly idea.

Harry Pointer thought that it would be funny to dress up cats as humans and take pictures of them with phrases superimposed underneath. By 1884, Pointer had amassed over 200 different cat photographs.

Still well before the advent of the Internet a scientist put out a book that would go on to shape our view of the World. In *The Selfish Gene*, originally published in 1976, Richard Dawkins coined the term "meme". At the time, he was describing the passing on of genetic code and how it affects our evolution. Little did he know that his term would take on a whole different meaning – something that everybody from friends to Internet jokesters to marketers would try to develop.

Around 130 years after Pointer's silly idea, on June 14th 2006, the domain lolcats.com was registered. The cat – unforgiving, sarcastic, selfish, playful, and angry – has become one of the most popular Internet memes. The images are funny and they make people smile, but so what? What can we learn from a 130+ year old story that involved a British photographer doing something funny, a scientist looking for the secrets to evolution, and some dude who struck gold by figuring out that people, for some reason, really, really, like to pass along funny pictures of cats to pass the time?

The common usage of the word "meme" describes an idea that spreads throughout the Internet. It can take on many different forms: it can be a picture, hashtag, video, hyperlink, or misspelled text. Memes spread virally and have been the subject of research by marketers because of their potential to create mass brand awareness.

But today I want to coin a new term – a term that builds upon Dawkins' original work – "the selfish meme." Simply put, it's an Internet meme that propagates selfishly. Every person that shares it is doing so for themselves, whether they know it or not. As you'll soon see, the response to perceived support from sharing these memes is physiological. When we do it we crave more, and the process spirals up. Every action that we take online is done

to make us feel that we are being viewed a certain way – that we're part of a group; that we're loved.

A share doesn't help business if nobody cares who the original creator was. I'd take it one step further and argue that a share doesn't do any good for the business if the meme isn't related to the business.

Nobody cares who creates a lolcats photo. It's cute and gets passed around before finding its rightful place in the deepest depths of the Internet.

What the Mesopotamians and Lolcats Have in Common

The ancient Mesopotamians are credited as the first people to build the arch, as far back as the 2nd millennium B.C. Since then the arch is one of the predominant structures spanning almost every culture.

The arch can span a wide-open space by applying a concept called 'arch configuration.' The shape becomes stronger with an increase in compression, and that has made it an invaluable tool for architects.

Perhaps the most important aspect of arches is that their concept can be applied to a wide variety of materials. The specifics don't matter; leave that to the engineers. The arch works. *The concept has stood the test of time.* Human desires bear a stunning resemblance: we have the same needs that we've always had (to feel loved, and be part of a group). We also want to laugh and smile – maybe that's why, 130+ years later, people are still passing along funny images of cats.

The World will change, but human behaviour won't. The biggest mistake that you can make is to attempt to keep up with new innovations before taking the time to understand *why* people use those innovations.

The only constant is that if you try, you'll be playing catch-up your entire career, and life. But, if you understand what motivates people to talk and to share then you can get them to talk and share with your goals in mind, regardless of the buttons they use.

This book won't tell you how much concrete to mix. This book will tell you how the arch works in order to empower you to use whatever tools, software, and buttons are at your disposal at the time so that you're always one step ahead.

These ideas aren't new.

"THERE ARE NO MAGIC TRICKS, POTIONS, OR SECRETS THAT YOU CAN BUY FOR $27."

- @jon_ptdc

Here's What is New...

Unless you live in isolation you're faced with an onslaught of marketing messages every day. It takes a lot of energy to put up a barrier to ignore them.

This exertion is exhausting, and we need a refuge. That refuge is social media.

Much has been said about the marketing benefit of social media related to finding, targeting, and communicating with your audience. To me, this benefit is secondary. We work hard every day to ignore marketing so that we can go home and put our feet up to relax. And when we do this, we go on social media. It's a place where our subconscious takes over. It's a place where we let our emotions dictate our actions. It's a place where we're more open to persuasion than anywhere else.

The benefits of this when attempting to build a platform, or influence to sell a product or service, are two-fold:

1. Persuasion techniques are more effective on social media than anywhere else.

2. If you know what to look for you can easily identify when a person is in a state of low emotional stability so that you know when to escalate the relationship and scale your efforts at adding value.

All that I ask is that you use the material in the following pages for good.

PART ONE:

THE CAST

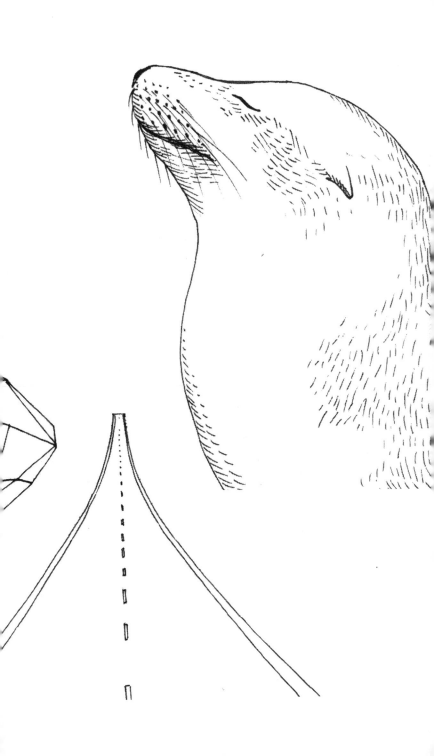

Who Are They?

As you navigate online social networks you're going to encounter some key characters. Understanding who the different cast members are, and knowing how to best use and serve them, is an important piece of the puzzle.
So let's meet them...

Carpenter Ants

You don't see carpenter ants. They prefer moist wood and usually reside in decks and porches. They dig nests in the wood and cut out galleries so they can move from nest to nest. Aside from being pests and occasionally leaving some sawdust around, carpenter ants don't do much real damage.

They just exist.

They use your home and never say thank you. Without you (or people like you) they wouldn't have a place to live.

I Was a Carpenter Ant

For two years, I secretly hollowed out blogs and didn't even think about giving anything back. I never "liked," shared, or tweeted a thing. It never crossed my mind to send a thank you note to the authors, and I never bought a thing from their sites.

Groggily, I'd wake up and put oil in the frying pan. As it heated I would turn on my computer and open my favourite blogs and websites. I perfected the technique of using one hand to eat my eggs so my other hand would stay clean to use the mouse.

Like a sponge, I absorbed and adapted much of what I read. Without these blogs my career would be years behind where it is now.

Most readers of your information are carpenter ants and they're hollowing you out from the inside. Without you they wouldn't survive, yet they don't give you anything in return.

Whether you work for a multi-national company, a small neighbourhood branch, or wish to improve your personal brand, carpenter ants are there. That's fine – you're helping them. The problem is that with only them you won't survive. Your success is solely dependant upon how successful you can make others. If they don't buy anything from you, they might know someone who will.

You'll always have carpenter ants but they aren't the key people that you need to help spread your message. What you need to identify are your road builders.

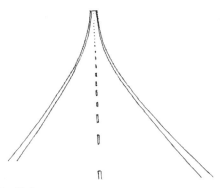

The Road Builder

Greg Ohnoez is one of my most important followers. He's not well known or particularly well-connected. For as long as I've known him, his Facebook profile picture has been a Buddha. When I spoke to him, he even told me that his real name wasn't Greg Ohnoez -- it's Greg O'Hare. I don't know what he looks like and, until recently, didn't know his real name. *Yet I have Greg O'Hare to thank for a lot of my success.*

Greg is somebody who is avidly interested in fitness. Out of nowhere, he entered the Internet fitness community and made an impact. He uses his page as a diary – as a way to organize his thoughts. He doesn't care if anybody else reads it, which is largely why people do. Through Facebook, Greg plays a large part in how information spreads throughout the fitness community. He gives power to many of the top figures in a powerful industry and he doesn't even know he's doing it.

Greg's goal is not to become famous and it's not to sell a product or service. He's a consumer and wants to talk about what he cares about and who he loves.

When Greg likes somebody or something, he shares it. Interact with Greg and he'll interact back. Show Greg O'Hare that he's important and he'll go out of his way to make sure his World knows who you are.

If your goal is to make an impact then find your own Greg O'Hares – my guess is they've been right under your nose the whole time.

The Sea Lion

My family was on a little fishing boat in the middle of Alaska. The water was calm when, out of the blue, birds started to congregate in one place. All of a sudden the sonar under our boat started broadcasting whale calls. Bubbles formed at the top of the water and 15 whales shot out. The once calm and idyllic setting turned into a flurry of activity with whales getting most of the krill fish.

What most wouldn't have noticed were the sea lions. The sea lions stayed on the outside of the chaos and caught the fish that the whales left behind or flung too far away.

They knew that by following the whales they'd have dinner.

Sea lions in Alaska are opportunistic.

Influencers have done the work for you. Their appeal and widespread respect have congregated lots of like-minded people in one place. When they post on Facebook or Twitter it starts a flurry of activity similar to a bubble feed.

Why not follow the sea lions' example?

Instead of trying to get the attention of the influencer during a bubble feed, why not use it as research? Pay attention to those commenting and liking the influencer's post. These are your targets – not the influencer.

I found Greg O'Hare by being a sea lion. He commented on three straight posts from three different influencers on the same day. It was obvious from the start that he was the type to actively participate and spread information. I found his network and built a relationship with him.

Success is achieved by finding those that are willing and eager to share, comment, and "like" your work. Not everybody will, despite your best efforts. The trick is to find your Greg O'Hares.

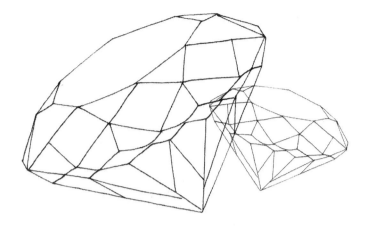

The Diamonds in the Rough

There are the influencers – but they actually don't matter that much.

Find the diamonds in the rough. These are the people behind the people and the publications that drive your network or neighborhood.

Want to gain influence? Become a sleuth. Who in the media has written about influential people in your industry? They are your targets. Find them, and identify the areas of their professional lives where they have the least amount of friction. There's always a place. Email is almost never it.

Bide your time watching these people, learning more about them. Wait for an opportunity to escalate the relationship.

Here are a few examples:

- **They will ask for help with a project they're working on.** When they ask a question that you can answer, respond right away with a recommendation, introduction, or by directly answering their question.

- **They are promoting a product, article or book.** Helping out with promotion out of the goodness of your heart is your best opportunity to escalate the relationship. If you listen well, you'll know a couple of weeks before your diamond is putting something out for sale. Message them and ask for an interview or if you can buy a preliminary copy for review. When they say yes, write the best review, article, or interview you can possibly write.

Once you're in, you're in. The hardest part is getting your first major break. Once you have it, use it to get more.

This book will show you how to attract, appeal to, and foster relationships with those who will share your info. It will teach you how to establish your network and create content to spread purposefully through it, finding more of your ideal consumers.

The Expert is "the Guy"

Everybody wants to know a guy. When somebody needs help with something, doesn't it feel good when you can say that you know the perfect person for that? Social capital rises from being able to help others by knowing an expert. Being able to refer the go-to person becomes a point of pride.

You need to become "the guy."

The go-to.

The resident expert.

This is scalable. There's a need for the guy for plumbing, the guy for furniture, the guy for fitness advice, and the guy for insurance. Whatever you do, there's a need for "a guy" and I suggest you make yourself the guy.

The guy doesn't necessarily know more than anybody else. Instead, the guy is able to be in the right place at the right time and has a knack for articulating the spoken and unspoken desires of others who share his or her expertise clearly, eloquently, and consistently, and becomes the voice of the network.

If you wish to become a trusted authority you need to know enough and be successful, but even more so you've got to have an ability to build a following: a following whose voice you understand and speak for.

It starts and ends with being true to yourself.

What do you stand for?

What do you know?

Draw a line in the sand. There will be those with you, and those against you.

The expert holds an unfathomable amount of power. The expert owns the feed.

You must become the expert. "The Guy."

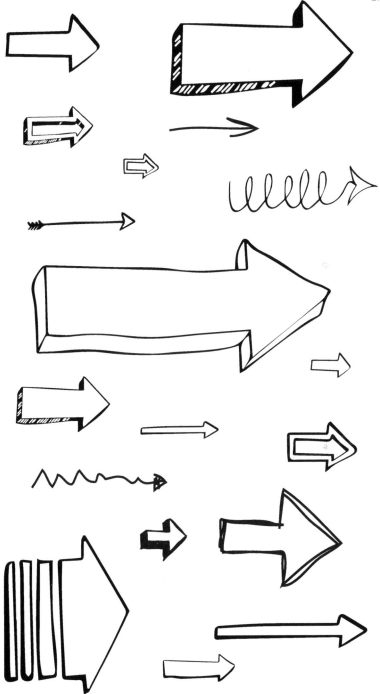

PART TWO:

WHAT'S GOING ON?

Why Are You Fighting What's Going On?

Most people think of marketing as a way of "doing something" to a consumer. The popular term today is persuasion – which just seems to be a nice way of saying "manipulation."

I suggest something different. Instead of attempting to convince or dupe an individual to do something out of the ordinary for them, why not simply facilitate a process already underway? Consumers have already aligned themselves in social groups based around things they like, don't like, and believe. Give them something to enhance their social World and perceived social standing in that World.

Mark Earls, author of Herd: *How to Change Mass Behavior by Harnessing Our True Nature* coined the term "curating diffusion" and recommends that we start talking about customers in the plural – that is, groups of people with similar interests, beliefs, and challenges.

Earls, in a 2010 paper for the *Marketing Society,* is quoted as saying: "Your job, in other words, is less about getting folk to do stuff and more about helping them to get each other to do stuff and so on through the population."

The previous passage holds the key. It's not about getting people to do something for themselves, it's about getting them to do something that they feel serves the population as a whole. Before showing you how to get people to want to do stuff that helps the community, propelling you to expert status, I want to discuss what's going on a bit more.

The Playing Field Has Become Levelled

Everybody in the same geographic location sees the same television commercial, or billboard, or sign but no two people see the same feed.

For the first time in history, an individual has the same opportunity to gain market share in a select audience as an industry giant. Every person selects who and what he or she wants to listen to in their feed.

All you have to do is get the right type of person to select you.

"THERE ARE THOSE WHO KNOW THE RULES OF WHAT IS POSSIBLE AND WHAT IS IMPOSSIBLE. YOU DO NOT. AND YOU SHOULD NOT." LOOSELY BASED OFF OF A QUOTE FROM NEIL GAIMAN

- @jon_ptdc

Filter Bubbles

Media theorist Marshall McLuhan once said, "We become what we behold. We shape our tools, and therefore our tools shape us."

A "filter bubble" originally described by Internet activist Eli Pariser in his book *The Filter Bubble*, which came out a few years before he formed *Upworthy*, the fastest growing website in history, describes the personalized search that results on websites. This happens because of algorithms that track everything from our age, gender and location to our behaviours across the Internet.

Amongst others, here are two results of the filter bubbles we, often unknowingly, create:

1. Confirmatory information becomes prevalent and dissuading information never gets seen. The result, in Pariser's own words, is that, "first, the filter bubble surrounds us with ideas with which we're already familiar (and already agree), making us overconfident in our mental frameworks. Second, it removes from our environment some of the key prompts that make us want to learn."

2. Loved ones dominate our feeds. If we interact with somebody, there's a good chance that we'll see more from him or her, and less from everybody else.

When a person that you trust links to a movie trailer, you watch it when you'd otherwise skip the commercial. When they tag a blog post as "something I found interesting" you read it more thoroughly than you would if you came across the same article via an organic search.

The feed is the most important aspect of your business. Gain access to it and build your networks within it using the ideas that I'm about to share with you. That, and owning a network is the most valuable asset you can have – it's probably worth more than any widget that you may sell.

Content used to be king, but it no longer matters. What matters now is that your content is packaged and positioned properly. Don't try to change people's minds right away. Instead, appeal to those who already agree with you or your position.

"YOU'VE GOT TO EARN YOUR SOAPBOX."

- @jon_ptdc

The Feed

The feed is the most important marketing tool. Those at the top will become the go-to sources for information in their community, their industry, and the World.

Miss out on the feed and you'll be pushed aside, not just from people's minds but also from their wallets. Feeds are turning into reverse search engines showing you what you want to see before you think to ask.

I believe:

- Referral traffic to websites will continue to grow making conventional SEO (Search Engine Optimization) less valuable.

- Those who understand what benefits individuals gain from sharing via social media will develop into industry experts earlier and with fewer credentials than ever before.

- Professional accounts don't dominate feeds. Large organizations will be forced to establish representative personalities.

- Perception of quality is more important than actual quality when attempting to get material to share.

Information is shared for three main reasons:

1. It's funny / nice to watch (usually useless to the creator unless the product for sale is low price and sold on fear/emotion or entertainment).

2. The person sharing wants to become part of a group or strengthen their position within one.

3. The person sharing is either consciously or sub consciously using the information to selectively self represent. This is driven by emotion.

The feed is an extension of personal relationships scaled almost infinitely. And it's where you should be focusing all of your resources. Why? Users trust the people providing information within their feeds.

We're starting to get into the fun part now, so let's keep going.

106,000,000

Search "SEO help" in Google and this is how many results you get. I went back as far as the 40th page and still found seemingly legitimate companies claiming to optimize your SEO with the promise to get you on the first page.

Would you go to an SEO company found on the 40th page of the search for help?

Promises of SEO help are everywhere. You can buy books on it in stores or download E-books from thousands of different sites. It seems to be the game that companies have to win in order to succeed in the modern day. Search engines are being used less and less and the quality of viewers from search engines is poor.

SEO is important for some. Depending on when you're reading this, local, niche businesses may still be able to make a mark with a bit of determined effort. Unfortunately, the fact is most web experts can make sure you have your tags in the right place and direct your content creation. And that's all I would suggest you have done.

Quality customers aren't the ones who'll find you through search. They'll be referred to you through the feed and offline word of mouth. People find what they're looking for by scanning their feeds or asking their friends.

They've pre-selected who and what they want to listen to. Getting in the feed is how you will win the next generation of business, not by gaming a search engine.

And if somebody finds you through a search engine you've still got to prove to him or her that you're "worth it." But if they get told from a friend that you're "the guy" for that, then the first question that they ask you quickly shifts from "why should I choose you?" to "how do I start?"

Search engines don't breed commitment - they breed carpenter ants.

The majority of people who find information via search engines are looking for specific information. They find an article, pick the specific information they need, and click off. They don't pay attention to the site or the author, and they definitely don't sign up for the newsletter. It's a need-to-know effort.

PART THREE:

STARTING TO PUT THE PIECES IN PLACE

Your Personal Network

Before you reach a position of influence (and even after you do) your personal social network on whatever platform you use is your most valuable business asset. Whether you met her once at a party or was introduced to him by a friend while playing golf, that person has reason to trust you more than anybody else in your industry.

Grow your network by adding every single person that you meet to whatever social network that you use. Remember that every person that you meet has their own network, and every person there has their own network. And if somebody knows somebody who knows somebody who needs a plumber, well... there's a guy for that. And you need to be that "guy."

You Should Waste More Time on Facebook

In the early 1900s there was an efficiency expert that excitedly walked into his boss' office exclaiming that he had made a discovery.

He spoke of an employee down the hall who was sitting with his feet on the desk and had been this way for some time. The expert advised his boss to fire the employee.

Henry Ford calmly responded to the efficiency expert by saying, "that man once had an idea that saved me a million dollars. When he got it, his feet were right where they are now."

The need to always appear "busy" is an issue that plagues society. Wasting time is frowned upon, rightfully so, but are we really wasting time on Facebook when we think we are? I, for one, don't think so.

In 1973 the American Journal of Sociology published a paper called *The Strength of Weak Ties*. It argued that success is more dependent on one's peripheral contacts and vague acquaintances than on one's closest friends. The paper went on to say that **one's close friends had almost nothing to do with one's success**.

Malcolm Gladwell's bestselling book*, The Tipping Point,* is based off of the study, and it is the reason why the girl that you met once at a party five years back that you haven't spoken to since but is a friend on Facebook is immensely valuable to you.

Vice President of Ogilvy UK Rory Sutherland says, "Facebook is about nothing if it is not about serendipity, coincidence, the happy accident, the shared admission— quite simply it's all about increasing one's chances of becoming the lucky victim of a happy accident."

Your chances of success start and finish with how lucky you get. Do everything that you can to increase your chances.

Many social media experts seem to be obsessed with the buttons: A/B testing Facebook ads, the "best" way to design a page, the best apps and so on. **The importance of the buttons pales in comparison to the ability to get your users to want to push them, and want to talk about you**.

Metcalfe's Law (established in 1993) states that the power of a network is directly correlated to the square of the number of nodes on that network. Marketing, any kind of marketing, is about staying at the top of someone's mind for long enough so that when they decide to buy, you're the first person they think of.

But mindless scrolling doesn't cut it.

Two things to do:

1. **Actively promote someone else every day**. It doesn't matter if they are in your industry or not. Have a friend in a band? Promote her show. Noticed that somebody you went to grade school with just wrote a blog post? Share word of it.

2. **Be consistent and always be helpful.** Post one tip or piece of advice relating to your area of expertise every day. The goal is simple ... every single person in your extended network needs to know what you do. Your success depends on whether or not you can stay at the top of the mind long enough so that when they, or somebody that they know, needs your service, product, or whatsinit, you're the one who gets the call.

This Happens When You've Become "the Guy"

One day I was procrastinating getting to work on this book and a Facebook notification popped up. Somebody tagged me in a fitness video that I hadn't heard anything from in years.

We went on one date in high school. I was probably 15.

For some reason I became Facebook friends with her some time in University. We never spoke.

I have no mutual friends with her anymore. Other than Facebook, there's no reason why she would ever know that I have anything to do with fitness. She has never commented, liked, or interacted with me on Facebook in any way. Nor have I interacted with her.

But I was the only person she tagged in a video she deemed funny about exercise. She thought of me when watching this video.

Unbeknownst to me she refers to me as "the fitness guy" for no reason other than I've posted about fitness stuff on Facebook.

What does this mean? Maybe nothing.

Or maybe, just maybe, she might, at some point, know somebody who knows somebody who went to dinner with somebody who wants to become a personal trainer and now will get told about my site, books, and courses.

This is the power of social networks. You can't measure this. This is scalable. This is an example of what will happen when you put yourself in the best possible position to catch a lucky break.

Professionalism and Privacy

You've likely been building up a profile, collecting friends, and adding content for years. This is now your business profile. Go through it and delete any party photos and any content that you deem unprofessional, whatever that means to you. From now on you will send a friend request using this profile to everybody you meet.

If you like, and what I've done, is to create a separate profile under a pseudonym. I sent a message to 40 or so of my very close friends and family and asked that they join me there. This is where I hang out. It's personal and it's maybe not quite as professional as my other account.

If I'm at a party I'll ask my friends or family to only tag the pseudonym account in pictures and I monitor my professional personal account (the one that uses my real name) closely.

The Business Professional Page

This is where you create your movement. It's a gathering point for your community.

Most business pages have very little feedback. They're a long list of posts, articles, or news releases that are ignored because nobody cares. They are impersonal and don't give anything to the reader. Having high numbers doesn't matter much. You need a critical mass so that if you do something that justifies sharing it will spread. Depending on your industry it will be 10,000-15,000. Once you have that, higher numbers on social media without a resulting growth in interaction (active users) and sales is a vanity metric and not something to strive for.

The biggest mistake that the owner of a business professional page can make is to put the focus on the business or brand and not on the message or idea that it represents.

Why does your company exist?

What does it stand for?

What are you passionate about?

Who are you against?

What are other things that fans of your page might be interested in?

This is what the focus of your page must be. Your products come second.

The Personal Trainer Development Center (the PTDC) is a collaborative blog for personal trainers that I own and operate. We sell information that helps personal trainers make more money, help more people, and have more freedom. Cool. None of that really matters when it comes to social media.

Here's what does:

The fitness industry is one of the most persuasive, dishonest, and untrusted industries in the World. It shouldn't be this way. Fitness is preventative health and personal trainers are at the forefront of the "exercise is medicine" movement that is our only hope for reversing obesity and dealing with overwhelming health care costs. The PTDC stands for integrity, honesty, and truth in an industry where deceit is omnipresent.

Broadcasting this message is why we've been successful on social media. You're either with us, or you're against us. Successful businesses are not those that just produce great products. They're ones that have customers who care about them and want to be a part of their movement.

Ideas share from business professional pages if the page articulates the desires of an audience, and a major way of doing this is by making them feel a part of your movement. Here's a sample of how I might share an article from the PTDC's business page:

"If you take personal training seriously you have to read this."

... and follow with an article about the importance of researching supplements properly before selling them.

The reason why I don't just link the article about supplements and include a line about the importance of research is that it wouldn't make me stand out. It wouldn't give a viewer any reason to pay more attention to me than the next guy.

There's going to be a lot of people saying similar things to you. Who are you for and who are you against? Always communicate that message. Your content supports it.

"EMOTION DRIVES ACTION. LOGIC JUSTIFIES IT."

- @jon_ptdc

250,000

Unknowingly, you've been building your customer list for as long as you've had Facebook. Some are close friends, some family, and some schoolmates you haven't seen for 20 years. These are your primary leads and your access point to thousands more. If I have 500 Facebook friends who all have 500 Facebook friends, that's 250,000 potential leads.

Unless you've already tapped this massive resource, don't start looking elsewhere to do your marketing. After all, these people already have at least one person in common with you and that is reason enough to trust you more than somebody else.

The trick is to avoid coming off spammy. Posting messages on people's walls or tagging people in notes so that it appears on their public wall will get your feed blocked – quick. Always add value.

Start with a simple "tip of the day" related to your industry. Make it short and include a soft call to action at the bottom of each. Simply post it on your wall. The best tips are personal and no more than 3-4 lines. Highlight the tip as your "_____ Tip of the Day" and end each tip with, "If you have any questions always feel free to contact me." Here's an example:

Fitness Tip of the Day: Skin care is much better accomplished from what you ingest then what you place on top of your skin. Drinking water, taking fish oil and eating healthy fats like avocado and raw nuts trumps moisturizers any day. Feel free to message me if you or a friend ever has any fitness-related questions.

Even if you don't get responses, your tips will start to resonate with your loved ones. Within weeks I promise you'll be the one contacted with questions related to your tips. When your friends are ready to buy a product you're selling they'll buy it from you. As an added bonus, they'll start sending you referrals if they hear of somebody interested in your business.

It's all a matter of becoming present in the feed through adding value, not spamming your product asking people to BUY NOW!

Encyclopedia Britannica

On March 13, 2012 Encyclopedia Britannica announced that, after 244 years, it would no longer be printing books.

I remember countless nights when I was young lying on the floor with a random volume I'd picked up off of the shelf. I distinctly remember leafing through Pa-Pj. One night, while flipping through the golden-trimmed pages, I came across a picture of a piranha. I spent the next hour learning every detail about piranhas.

Information used to be so valuable its edges were golden. Adults would buy books on instalments because they couldn't afford to pay for the collection up front. They'd proudly line their shelves with an Encyclopedia as a sign of an educated household.

The joy wasn't in finding the answer. *The joy was in the search.*

Times changed and information became cheap. The CD-Rom compressed a collection of books into a disc that was portable. All of a sudden information lost its lustre. Clicking on a computer can never replace leafing through a meticulously crafted book. Information gathering became a need-to-know activity and learning ceased to be fun. A project was assigned, a mouse was clicked, and a plagiarized paper was handed in.

In a few short years CD burners came out, browsing speed increased, and online storage space grew. Wikipedia gave free access to more information than any one person would ever need and bloggers all over the World started publishing their thoughts for free. Information that was once cherished quickly became ignored.

Information is no longer valuable.

What you have to say is being said for free by thousands of other people on the Internet. The honest truth is that unless you're a leading researcher you have nothing profound to offer in terms of content.

The key to success is how you position and package your information. How much do your readers connect with you, the author, and what will they gain by passing on the information? The battle for content is over; anybody can rehash the facts.

Content's Fall From Grace

Content used to be King. Once it became abundant, context took over.

Now content with proper context isn't enough. You've got to become a master at packaging and positioning your information.

Make it good.

Know who it's for.

Know how "they" benefit from it.

"Hook" them with that benefit right away.

Dress it up so that it's clear to read, simple to understand, easy to benefit from, and the next steps are clearly laid out.

"CONTENT" IS WHAT'S USED TO FILL THE SPACE IN-BETWEEN ADVERTISEMENTS. DON'T PRODUCE "CONTENT". CRAFT VALUE."

- @jon_ptdc

The Newest, Oldest, Drug on the Market

There's a hip drug on the market and everybody, yes, even you, is addicted.

This drug gives us a shot of dopamine, the feel good hormone. When we get it, we crave more. We spend our days seeking out our next hit.

I call this drug "IIIAF".

This drug controls our minds. It manipulates our actions and affects our interpretation of events. It is the newest, oldest, drug on the market. Only this drug doesn't come as a pill and it's not injected. It's invisible to the eye.

Every action that's taken online is driven by the powerful desire to appear

Intelligent

Intellectual

Interesting

Attractive

Funny.

The most interesting aspect of this drug is that whether we actually *are* these things is irrelevant. You will get your fix if you *believe* others perceive you as IIIAF. If I think that you think that I'm smart, I get a shot of dopamine and I feel good even if you actually think that I'm stupid.

IIIAF is selective self-representation.

IIIAF is why people share pictures of their food; it's the reason for selfie-photos; and is the reason that, in an increasingly impersonal society, we'll continue to give up our privacy and let down our barriers to marketing messages in order to get our fix.

IIIAF is also the most powerful marketing tool at your disposal.

Selective self-representation isn't anything new. It's been spoken about in psychological research for years and appeared in relation to computer-mediated communication as early as 2007. If you know what to look for, the desire for perceived social-support is omnipresent.

The easiest way to see what personal or professional attribute a person lacks confidence in is to pay attention to what they boast about. Boasting is a compensatory behaviour. A confident person doesn't need to boast.

In a qualitative study performed in 2011, 569 Facebook users were asked why they shared a status update that they later regretted. Some users admitted to being inebriated, but the overwhelming conclusion was that regretful status updates were published when the sharer was in a state of emotional instability. The status update was created to provide them with a hit of perceived social support.

Also important to note is that few have the confidence to start the conversation themselves. In 2010 only 15% of Facebook users reported updating their status daily. People want to be heard, but they need a voice to articulate their thoughts and desires for them. This is where you come in.

While the desire to gain perceived support for things that we're unconfident about hasn't changed, the advent of the Internet (and social media in particular) has made two notable changes:

1. It's thrust into our faces all day, every day. Much has been said about the addictive nature of social media. It's on our phones and increasingly everywhere and everything seems to be trying to become social. My GPS just asked me to rate Costco as I pulled out of the parking lot. If I had accepted it would have asked me to share my rating on Facebook. We can't get away.

2. The age of asynchronicity. When I speak to somebody in-person or on the phone it's a synchronous conversation. You speak, I respond. I don't have much time to weigh, both consciously and unconsciously, the effect of my response or, and perhaps more importantly, how I believe my response is going to have me viewed.

With text messaging, instant messaging, and comments on social networks, many now live in a World where asynchronous communication is primary. You talk and I take as much time as I desire to respond. I have as much time as I want to craft a message in an attempt to get whatever perceived response serves me best. The importance of this point for establishing influence and power over a desired network cannot be overstated.

At a time when we have the entire combined knowledge of all human innovation in a device kept in our pocket and an overwhelming stream of new information being produced every minute, you'll soon learn that silence...

...IS PART OF THE MUSIC.

Duck Lips and Selfies Aren't All That Interesting but...

...When you consider that people who crave social support (those who rank lower on scales of emotional stability), often in the way of "likes," are more prone to negative health habits such as over-eating, smoking, and drinking as compensatory behaviours, the story begins to get more interesting.

The interplay between areas of study is where patterns begin to emerge that bear mention.

Social psychology isn't all that interesting, but when you look at the carry-over to physiology it becomes a neat field to study. Now add fuel to the fire by adding in an element of behavioural economics and you start to see how all of the seemingly benign behaviours that happen online represent the bigger picture of what's going on. The shape of how to use these things to gain trust and build relationships then spreads.

Almost all of us have a deep-rooted physiological desire to feel accepted, both online and offline. Compensation occurs when something isn't being met. So while duck lips (that weird pouty face people make that's meant to look cute or sexy, I think, I'm not really sure) and selfies aren't all that interesting, they represent a bigger, more important picture. These behaviours are a sign that the person is reaching out for support. They're a sign that the person is missing an element in their everyday life or relationships.

Not only does social media make sharing less threatening, but the response to sharing online versus offline will almost always be much greater, leading to more perceived support. Learning to identify the times when your friend group is reaching out for help and being the one to provide it will put you in a powerful position. That, and you might just stop the person from smoking a cigarette later.

The Engineer

"A good engineer takes pride in being lazy for he then creates systems that do not need constant meddling with."

- Unknown

There will always be something new and exciting.

Pundits will try to convince you that the *next best thing* is the better way. And it might be. Or it might be a worse way. Or the same.

Here's what is important:

You need to create systems that don't need trifling with and that cannot be affected by advances, innovations, widgets, or shiny whathaveits that come out. Base these systems off of building relationships, offering value, and establishing a power position.

Jon Goodman is...

Perhaps I'm dating myself, but I remember when Facebook status updates were really about what you were doing at that point in time. Facebook forced the word "is" after your name. How about Facebook groups? Remember them? Lots of companies do. Businesses spent piles of money building up their group members before Facebook decided to change to the professional page format in October 2010. Group members weren't transferred to the new pages and companies around the world lost millions of customer leads.

Pages gave companies the opportunities to design Apps. This started a new industry of Facebook App design and the race to get the best landing page was on. Lo and behold, Facebook decided to change its page format to a timeline on March 30, 2012. Apps were pushed to the side and their effectiveness went down.

Facebook, Twitter, Linkedin, and Pinterest will change. They may not even be relevant when you read this. Companies like Snapchat will pop up and try to make their mark. There will always be new social networks competing for your attention. If you try to keep up with all of the current trends and software you'll go nuts. Lucky for you it doesn't matter.

All you need to know is the answer to one simple question, "**Why do people share?**" It doesn't matter whether they "like," "tweet," "email," "check in," or "pin". The concept is the same. People are projecting where they are, who they want others to think they are, and what they want others to think they like. The trick is to make them speak about you using whatever means they have.

Buttons will change. The reasons people will push them won't.

Do you want to be a vet or an animal doctor?

Walking by a bus shelter a year ago, I saw an advertisement for a children's educational program that was supposed to be cute. It featured a cartoon image of a child saying to her mother:

"When I grow up I want to be a vet. That, or an animal doctor."

I expect that the goal of the ad was two-fold:

1. To get a smile from people passing by because a vet and an "animal doctor" are the same thing.

2. To appeal to parents who want their children to be successful.

But what this did for me is highlight one of the oldest and worst questions asked by almost every adult to almost every child. That question is:

"What do you want to be when you grow up?"

No child has the faculty to answer this question properly. Their experiences are too small.

The problem isn't just that children don't know what they want to be. It's that, in asking them the question and forcing an answer, they begin to identify with a certain profession early on before they've had the time to see and experience enough of the World to have any idea of what it is that they really want.

Information is abundant. We can learn anything within a matter of seconds. This is incredible.

But it requires one skill.

Learn to ask good questions.

This book is about learning *why* people use various networks and how you can use that information to appeal to your ideal consumers and get them to gain from promoting you.

That's a good question.

What is the best type of image to use as a Facebook cover photo, though, that's a terrible question.

"THE QUESTION BEING ASKED IS RARELY THE REAL QUESTION."

- @jon_ptdc

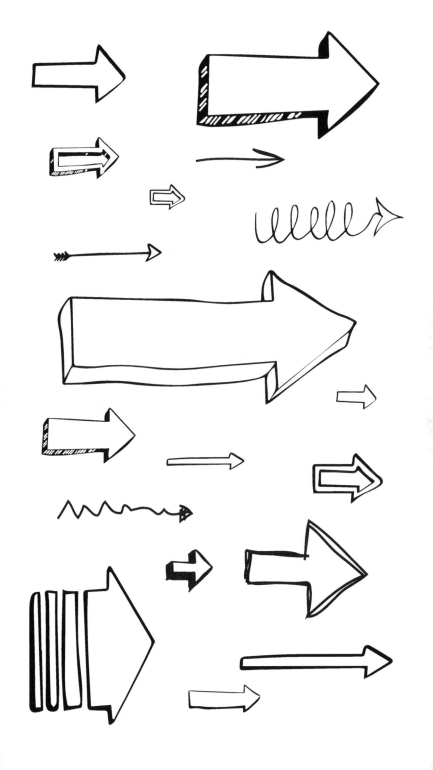

PART FOUR:

INFLUENCE

What is True Power?

There are two things to consider when building true power:

1. True power doesn't come from knowing. It comes from knowing where to find.

Two of the biggest websites in the World today, Reddit and Google, are built around a model of helping you find what you're looking for as fast as possible and leaving the site. The result? The sites become trusted. People come back. And people refer the sites to others. Become an information hub by helping people find what they're looking for and you'll become an integral, and influential, part of your community.

When somebody asks you a question about an aspect of your industry that you're not an expert in, you should know somebody who is, and "tag out". Doing this both strengthens your position as the go-to for information and provides the expert who you tagged with social equity.

I'm reminded of a fable involving Henry Ford. In 1919 he was involved in a slander lawsuit as a result of being called an "ignorant anarchist" in the Chicago Tribune. And, while Ford was originally most upset about the term "anarchist," the defense focused on the charge that Ford was an "ignorant idealist."

The lawsuit became bitter as Ford's opposition attempted to prove that he was ignorant. Court transcripts became popular after it became obvious that Ford didn't know the basics of American history (he thought that the revolutionary war happened in 1812 when it actually happened in 1775).

So was Ford stupid? If you judge him solely by what he knew about history, maybe. But Ford knew that what he knew didn't matter much. What mattered was that he had the resources to find the answers when he needed them.

Build a formidable network of experts in all different topics around yourself. It doesn't matter much that you know. What matters is that you *know where to find.*

2. True power is maintaining a position of control where everybody owes you one, and not vice-versa.

Go out of your way to do favours for people. Recall an earlier section where I showed you how to identify when somebody is in a low state of emotional stability. Be the one to support them when they are reaching out for help. Promote her book when she releases it. Share word of his new company when he makes an announcement.

Spend time every day looking for ways to do as many favours as possible. You'll soon realize that these favours take very little time, effort, and money, and have fantastic rewards. All it takes is the ability to appeal to emotion and, as you'll soon see, stay at the top of mind as often as possible by linking you or your company in with something that is important to the other person.

This is not an overnight process; you won't see immediate rewards.

If you do five to ten people favours every day (and a favour could be as small as congratulating him when he releases a book and sharing word of it on your Facebook) then you'll soon find yourself in a position of power. And this position cannot be touched because, in the words of my friend and creator of *MastermindTalks,* Jayson Gaignard, "deep down inside I knew in the worst case, that the bank could take my car, they could take whatever measly assets I had left, but they couldn't take my network."

Why All Free Samples Should be Served With a Metal Spoon

My girlfriend and I were famished after a workout and decided to get some food.

In front of a green sign there stood two girls, somewhere around 20 years old, dressed in black slacks and white button up blouses with a tray. On the tray was a collection of tiny paper cups, the kind they use to offer free samples of food. As we approached, one girl said "tiramisu?"

We both grabbed a paper cup and looked at the dessert, it wasn't finger food and needed a utensil.

"Want a spoon?" The second one asked.

I picked up a metal spoon, gave the customary "thank you," and started to walk away but immediately stopped myself. They got me. *I was trapped.*

The goal of giving away a free sample is to let a passerby try your food and buy something. Most times, though, I don't even know the name of the food or restaurant I'm sampling. If she gave me a plastic spoon I would have walked away without a second thought.

But convention says that I needed to return the metal spoon. I was forced to stay. Staring at each other, I asked about the restaurant. She told me that it was a vegan, gluten free, Italian restaurant that just opened.

Vegan, gluten-free Italian food is NOT a thing. Gnocchi doesn't mean lentils wrapped in lettuce. Sorry.

But we were already committed and hungry, so my girlfriend and I walked in and had lunch. Thirty-four dollars later, we waved goodbye to the girls as we left.

Well-played blouses. Well-played.

When developing your message, it's not a matter of how many buttons you push or how many messages you put out, what matters is that you push the exact right button at the exact right time.

Think – what is it that your reader or prospect wants right now? What word or phrase will stop him or her in her tracks? What is *the one thing* that will appeal to them right now based off of how they feel, what they already have, and what they desire?

If you do it right you might just convince a carnivore to spend 34 dollars on lettuce-wrapped lentils.

As Few Steps as Possible

Always consider your reader's state of awareness. What is it that he or she wants to know?

Reduce the number of steps as much as possible to help them get precisely what they want.

An example? Instead of posting your website address in your Twitter or Facebook profile link directly to the about page on your site. If a user has taken the effort to check out your profile you've gotten that buy-in, now they want to know about you and what you can do for them.

Put yourself in their head. Take them by the hand. Guide them to what they want to see.

The Secret to Selling at a Thai Market

In a hippie town called Pai in Thailand there is a large market that opens every night. It has everything that you'd expect from an Asian market – street food, cheap clothing, and unique jewellery that isn't unique at all.

In the middle of my effortless market walk where I'm not quite bored but not quite not bored, I notice that one booth has a crowd of people buying. We stayed in Pai for three nights and every night was the same. This one booth had a constant crowd while the others didn't.

I investigated. Why did this one booth that sold the exact same junk as the others seem to fare better?

After fighting my way through the throng of tourists earnestly buying up the "limited quantity" inventory (that would, of course, be replaced with more limited quantity goods soon after), I was surprised to find that not only was this booth selling the same chintzy jewellery, but also it was selling it at a higher price.

So what was going on?

The booth looked different than the others. It had a gold embroidered wall around it. The owners were smart enough to realize that if they invested a few dollars in creating the illusion of higher quality (called "trappings") then they could sell the same goods for more money.

Seeing this reminded me of a quote from Nobel Prize winner Daniel Kahnamen: "people consider a particular value for an unknown quality before estimating that quality."

In this particular instance, selling cheap – which is what most of the other booth owners did – was having the opposite of the effect. The tourists buying the goods would reason that the more expensive price was cheap compared to what they would pay at home.

What do your prospects really desire?

How can you dress up your product so that you stand out in a crowded marketplace, sell more, and charge more?

"TRUSTING WHAT THEY'RE BUYING ISN'T CRAP AND THAT THEY AREN'T GETTING RIPPED OFF ARE MOST PEOPLE'S STRONGEST MOTIVATORS."

- @jon_ptdc

It's an Information Onslaught

In 2003, Google CEO Eric Schmidt said that every two days we create as much information as human beings did from the dawn of civilization up until 2003. Since 2003 this process has compounded. I suspect that now this is happening every few hours.

More and more consumers are frustrated by the endless and often incomprehensible amount of information on the Internet. In Schmidt's words, "the real issue is user-generated content." This means that anybody with a keyboard and Internet connection can write about whatever they like. It's becoming increasingly difficult to "vet" sources and know who is right, who is wrong, and who is downright nutty.

Your quality product is getting lost in a sea of noise. Even if you're good, and I assume that you are, you risk being bunched in with people who aren't-so-good.

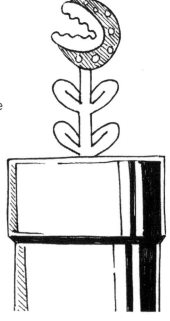

The old school method was to create more and more good content and possibly break through. That ship has sailed. Now you've got to create trust. You've got to master word-of-mouth. And, this may surprise you, but most of it still happens offline.

If somebody needs a plumber they're increasingly going to the feed because they trust the sources providing the information. It's easier putting a post on Facebook asking, "Anybody know a good plumber?" than calling 15 of your friends or leafing through the Yellow Pages. Better yet, the post reaches a percentage of all 500+ of your Facebook friends while your phone call only reaches a few.

A plumber's job then becomes getting to the top of the feed for that friend group and staying there until somebody that they know needs work done.

My guess is that the plumber already has a strong friend network in the neighbourhood where they work. Why not start releasing a "Plumbing Tip of the Day" on Facebook? Make them quick tips that any homeowner can use immediately after reading. Have a call to action at the end asking the reader to contact you with any questions. Twice a week, write a funny anecdote about plumbing on your website.

Be useful. Stop trying to impress other plumbers and get back to the basics. What you'll quickly find is that other plumbers will be more prone to share your simple plumbing tips rather than the more complicated ones. Attempt to make it time-sensitive as much as possible. For example, information on how to prepare your pipes for winter is perfect just before it gets cold.

In a study done by the Pew research center in 2011, 15% of Facebook users reported updating their own status at least once a day while 68% reported commenting or liking an update shared by somebody else. Even if the other plumbers are technically your competition, there's a good chance that they will share your post simply because it's easier than creating their own.

Search for pages that already service your target market and send your funny anecdote to them. Page owners consistently need new content. They won't all share it, but some will and now you've got an audience of plumbers who read and spread your content to reach more potential buyers. And remember the key to staying in the feed longer is not to appeal to potential customers; it's to articulate the desires of people that already think the same way as you. Don't market to people who need plumbing every day. Stay in the feed by appealing to handy-men and plumbers.

The other piece of the puzzle is to become the centre of information for your industry. Still with my plumbing example, for absolutely no reason, find all of the plumbing or handy-men blogs on the Internet and scan them (or hire somebody to scan them) and post a weekly list of the "best home maintenance articles." Email/message everybody featured.

This does two things:

1. People featured will share the weekly list because it makes them look good to get mentioned. The list is on your site. Remember?

2. You build a relationship with all other information providers in your industry based around your doing them favours. There's no better way to establish a power-position.

Soon, handy homeowners will share your tips. All of a sudden your value and reach grows. This process compounds until you're the go-to for plumbing in your neighbourhood (and beyond).

Anytime someone is looking for a plumber in your expanded network they'll ask the friend who'd posted a tip about plumbing months earlier. Their friend will quickly send over your name. *All because you've been able to stay in the feed until a potential customer needs your services.*

Based off of what we've spoken about so far, I have two conclusions of note:

1. Those who can figure out how to stay in the feed longer, not by trying to appeal to potential customers but by appealing to those who already agree with them, will win.

2. We've entered the age of the coach. The most valuable asset that any marketer can have is not to provide information, but to become a trusted entity so that they become "the guy" when someone is looking for a solution to their *specific problem.*

Emotion is Faster than Thought

In *How We Decide,* Jonah Lehrer says, "emotional sharing creates a bond between narrator and audience."

Emotion drives action; logic justifies it. Target emotion first. To target emotion, identify the benefits of your product or service.

The feed is fast. Attention spans are short. There's a lot going on. You've got to appeal to people right away or miss out. This means that you might need to bend without breaking. The point of your first sentence or first point is to give you an opportunity to make a second.

Every piece of marketing material that you put out, and this includes everything from independent status updates, to marketing materials, to a follow-up email series, needs to include the following three attributes in order:

1. Emotion/benefits
2. Value/steps to solving
3. Logic/features

How do you identify the benefits / emotional triggers of your product or service?

In his 1993 book *How to Make a Whole Lot More Than 1,000,000 Writing, Commissioning, Publishing and Selling How to Information,* Dr. Jeffrey Lant lists the 10 benefit categories of any product:

- Financial stability
- Health
- Love
- Security
- Salvation
- Self-regard
- Community and peer recognition
- Independence
- Sexual Fulfillment
- Beauty/desirability/personal attractiveness

Tap into one or more of the above benefits with every "ask" you make to increase your chances of gaining a lead or sale.

What are the action steps / value?

Here you give valuable information that helps your prospect solve their problem. It's an odd phenomenon, but solve somebody's problem for free and they will pay you to solve their problem.

How do you identify the logic / features of your product or service?

The features are components of your service that set it apart from the competition. Things like the specifications of your product vs. the competition, for example. In his 1976 classic, *Breakthrough Advertising,* Eugene Schwartz lists all of the possible pieces of logic or trust elements including:

- Proof
- Statistics
- Testimonials
- Quotes from authority figures
- Tests
- Trends (i.e. social proof)
- Seals of approval/authority
- Awards won

People Love Easy More Than They Like Cheap

Don't hide your price. Don't make your customers go in circles in order to buy.

Make it easy, but don't make it cheap.

The Formula

Every good status update follows the same basic formula:

1. Headline
2. Lede
3. Steps to solving
4. Call to action

The headline: This is what grabs the attention of your prospect. Make it short, hit on the biggest emotional benefit, and possibly use text decoration to stand out. Putting words like [Brand New] in brackets grants you an extra split second, which is usually enough for your reader to scan your headline and see whether it appeals to him or her.

Make a list of your favourite popular websites and go through their archive, creating a list of their most popular articles. Keep all of those headlines in a spreadsheet. When it comes time for you to write a new piece, see if any of the headline templates work and slip in wording specific to your piece.

Lede: 1-2 sentences that act as an introduction for the status that entices the reader to continue. Read any newspaper and you'll notice that a headline and lede are present in almost every article. Many websites, mine included, separate the lede in large font above the article body.

Steps to solving: Give a little bit of information. Ideally here you'll give something that the reader can immediately implement to have a positive effect. Lists work well to organize your steps to solving.

Call to action: If you want the sale, or a comment, or for them to join your newsletter, or something else, ask for it. Ideally you'll include the word "because," which, by the way, is the most powerful word in the English language. Adding a "because" statement helps somebody justify taking action to themselves. So instead of saying, "join my newsletter by clicking here." Say, "join my newsletter by clicking here because if you don't do anything today, how will tomorrow be any different?"

There's a huge variety of status updates. They vary in length and detail. This overview is a good formula to follow and, like any formula, you've got to know the rules before you can decide where to break 'em.

Respect Cognitive Ease

Consider the following two statements. Which is true?
  1. The Hoover Dam was completed in 1938.
  2. The Hoover Dam was completed in 1934.

Just writing words isn't enough. You've got to write words that people will believe. In his book *Thinking, Fast and Slow*, Nobel prize winner Daniel Kahnamen showed that we have a tendency to believe and trust information that's easier to process.

If a statement is easier to read, it's more believable. Using tools like bold, all capitals, and symbols [like this] that highlight certain text to make it easier to read reduces cognitive strain and makes your information easier to read and, as a result, increase the perception of believability.

Daniel Oppenheimer, in his brilliantly titled study "Consequences of Erudite Vernacular Utilized Irrespective of Necessity: Problems with Using Long Words Needlessly," also showed that the less jargon and needlessly complex wording you use, the more believable you are considered to be.

Respect cognitive ease. Keep it short and simple, avoid jargon and make yourself appear more trustworthy by appropriately using symbols to highlight your point.

Oh, and both statements above are false, the dam was completed in 1936.

But if You Want More Sharing...

There are two purposes to a status update: one is a call to action and the previous formula is a good one to follow. The other, well, I'm going to tell you a toilet story to illustrate it.

Close to my old condo in Toronto there's a Starbucks Coffee shop that is perfect to work in. The upstairs is outfitted with big wooden tables, there's lots of light, and it's always quiet. I used to go there to work when I got tired of my home office.

After a bottle of water, double espresso, and two hours or so I'm ready to leave, but first, need to use the toilet. So I pack up my stuff and head downstairs, walk down the short narrow hallway and see the two doors. I push the first, locked. Somebody sheepishly says "occupied." I push the second, it opens, WHAM, somebody pushes it back shut. They forgot to lock it.

So I lean up against the wall waiting for either of them to finish and exit. When they do, we exchange an awkward smile – the kind that only happens when neither person wants to smile but both people feel bad not smiling.

My final experience before leaving that Starbucks is not a positive one. I know that it seems like I'm battling in the minutia, but the last impression that you leave on somebody shapes their emotional opinion of you.

Now imagine if the person who designed Starbucks had the littlest foresight and put those locks on the door that show green when it's open, and red if it isn't. Airplanes have got this figured out. It would remove the awkwardness of having to check whether the stall is occupied and, for the person inside doing his or her business, they wouldn't get the door pushed on them.

Emotional sharing is what pushes content online. The last line of whatever message you create needs to stir something in your reader. It could be food for thought, a strong quote, a smile, or it could make him or her angry.

Why Do People Comment?

Read through the comments in a thread on any public network and you'll notice a pattern: few care about adding to the conversation or providing helpful advice – most use it to show off what they know (or what they think they know).

Even on the rare occasion when you write something that, gasp, people actually agree with on the Internet, the responses are almost never "great work" but instead "so true" or a sentence or two about how the person already knows and agrees with you.

Aside from pointing out the phenomenon, understanding that comment threads are yet another place where people want to show off what they want others to know about them should help you figure out what types of material to post and what responses to expect.

That, and the importance of respecting cognitive dissonance should shape how you interact with your audience. So let's talk about that for a minute.

On Responding to Comments Online

If the comment is happening on your platform, then it's a power struggle and you start with the advantage. If you're not careful you risk giving up that advantage quickly. Take time to consider your responses and, perhaps more importantly, who you're attempting to influence when responding, and how it will make you appear.

First, never engage in debates on platforms where the majority of the onlookers are of a differing opinion. Always aim to take the conversation to a platform that either you own or is neutral.

According to the seminal observational study of cognitive dissonance, *When Prophecy Fails,* the "believer" having "social support" is one of the most important contributors to "increased fervour following the confirmation of belief."

Even if you're right, debating somebody on a platform

where they will get the majority of support will actually strengthen their confirmation, having the opposite effect of your intention.

But comments can prove a powerful ally for strengthening your platform and expert status. Here's how:

Step 1: Always maintain composure and stay devoid of emotion. He or she who acts emotionally loses.

Step 2: Comment not to convince your combatant that he or she is wrong. Comment for the onlookers to convince those on the fence to come over to your side, strengthen your connection with those already with you, and further push away those who are against you.

I'll explain how this is done in practice in a minute. Before that, allow me to say that the perception of expertise is more important than actual expertness online. It's a sad reality and I hope that you use the following for good. Only profess to be an expert if you're actually an expert because you can easily lead people astray.

If you were to listen to an imbecile from England speak with a rocket scientist from Arkansas then, at first glance, without weighing the evidence, the imbecile would likely appear more intelligent. First glances are often all that you get online.

Earlier in this section I hit on the importance of speaking without emotion. Write full, grammatically correct sentences. Respect the rules of logic. In a sense, "sound" more intelligent than your combatant. He or she will become increasingly agitated, emotional, illogical, and, as a result, discredit him or herself.

Next, choose your time of attack. In your industry I'm sure that controversial subjects exist. Your desired audience will agree with one point. Your job with your comment responses is to appeal to those who you want to appeal to and repel all others.

So scan the comments in a thread on your platform and look for one that opposes a viewpoint that you agree with. Take as long as you need to compose a full, well-thought out, and well-articulated response. Post it once, and leave. Never engage in back and forth because if you do, you lose power. If you've done a good job two things will happen:

1. Your comment will have many more "likes" than the original comment.

2. Your combatant will get agitated and reply nonsensically and people who support him or her will do so in kind.

"THOSE WHO HAVE GROWN TO ATTAIN A STABLE POSITION OF POWER HAVE DONE SO THROUGH TRAINED CONTROL OF THEIR EMOTIONS."

- @jon_ptdc

Critics, Trolls, and Haters

You could be the nicest, most caring, most kind, and most giving person on the planet – but somebody on the Internet is still going to call you a jerk (or, in my case, a "racist, sexist, communist pig who hates America." Yes, that's a direct quote.) There are three negative characters that will pop up as you build your own platform. Here's how you identify and deal with each:

The Critic: Usually well-spoken. The critic is respectful of what you say but offers a differing opinion. They don't fall into the emotional trap and seemingly want to offer some help.

The critic helps you grow. All of us make mistakes and we're never right 100% of the time. Listen to what the critic says and figure out whether it's warranted or not. Perhaps you were actually wrong ... it happens and there's nothing wrong with it, that is, unless you refuse to admit it and change ways.

The Troll: These are people who take enjoyment in attempting to agitate others on the Internet. You can usually identify them because they make up their own words and often share a host of picture memes.

The best thing to do with the troll is to simply ban them from all of your networks. Don't respond; it's what they want. Ban them on social media, put them on the blocked list so they don't receive your emails, and block their IP (Internet Protocol) address from commenting on your website.

The Hater: No matter what you do, the hater will figure out a way to hate. They hold a grudge and take everything that you say as a personal affront to them. The main way to tell the difference between a hater and a troll is that the hater doesn't appear to make any effort to seem funny.

Use the hater to strengthen the conviction of your existing followers. He or she will be emotional and discredit him or herself quickly. Follow my steps in the previous section and don't give any thought to what haters say.

"I MAKE STUFF UP. IF IT WORKS, I KEEP IT AND IMPROVE UPON IT. ONCE IT STOPS WORKING, I FIGURE OUT SOMETHING ELSE. IF PROVEN WRONG, I CHANGE."

- @jon_ptdc

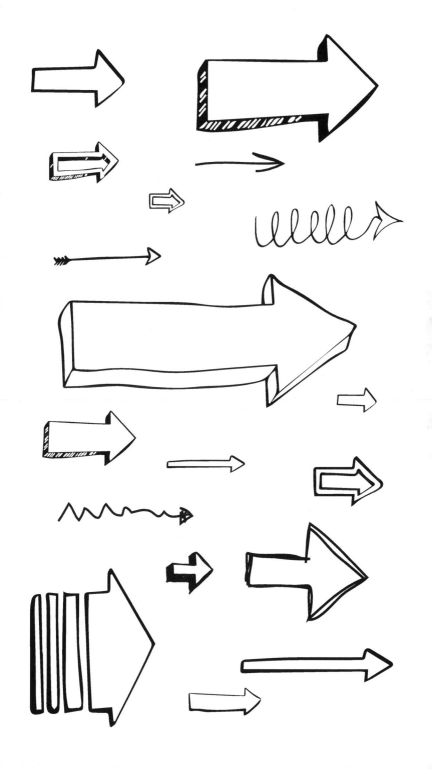

PART FIVE:

TACTICS

Diminishing Sensitivity

A dim light in a dark room gets noticed. A bright light in an already lit room gets ignored.

To stand out you don't need to yell louder, you just need to find the dark room.

People Aren't That Interested in You

First and foremost, online communities are a place to hang out. Continually posting information about your coffee shop is a sure-fire way to get your feed ignored and possibly blocked.

Write about your fair-trade coffee once a day. Spend the rest of the time gaining relevance. Or better yet, write about a relatable funny or interesting story that happened in your coffee shop.

People aren't all that interested in your coffee but aficionados love talking about interesting facts surrounding coffee, stories about the growers, the health benefits of it, and learning about the different variations. That, and if they are interested in fair-trade they are probably interested in other aspects of sustainable farming or healthy eating. Your business simply goes along for the ride.

The "like" button (or whatever Facebook has changed it to when you're reading this) is everything. It dictates relevance. Once you "like" a post, both the subject of the post and the person who posted it becomes more relevant to you.

When I was growing my fitness brand I recognized that people didn't care so much about my fitness business, but the ones I was interested in loved showing off that they were somehow involved in the fitness industry or had a healthy lifestyle.

When I realized that I stopped posting about myself. Instead I started sharing a healthy diet of jokes, motivational quotes, thought-provoking stories, and/or personal funny/relatable stories. All were related to my primary goal – to become the guy for fitness even if they don't mention a thing about training.

Here are examples of similar messages, each written from a different angle:

Fitness: "The best personal trainers are those that realize the job is an art – not a science."

Funny joke: "I was in the gym today and couldn't figure out what that buzzing sound was all around me. Then it hit me – I was doing dumbbell flys."

Motivational quote: "Well, it may be all right in practice, but it will never work in theory." – Warren Buffet

Thought-provoking or feel-good story: "Today my client told me that she used a ladder to get a plate off the top shelf. I didn't realize why it was a big deal. Then she repeated, "I got on a ladder." She went on to tell me that she hadn't been able to walk up a ladder in 20 years. It's not all about number goals, people. Sometimes the ah-ha moments are more meaningful than weight loss can ever be."

Personal/funny/relatable story: "I fell down the stairs at the gym today. Maybe that extra set of squats was a bad choice yesterday. Wow, my legs are sore. Anybody else train legs this week?"

The result was that I had people, some of whom I hadn't spoken to in as much as 15 years, messaging me and asking me for more information pertaining to my training services. I was referred family members and I started to get called in to provide quotes for newspapers and magazines simply because somebody who I knew from somewhere knew somebody who wrote for the newspaper. You can't measure this stuff but the better you put yourself in a position to catch a lucky break the more often it will happen.

The goal is to appeal to as many people as possible but not lose sight of your focus. Different people will "like," click on, and share different types of materials.

This is where many large companies that use metrics to dictate success go wrong. Their research tells them that one type of information shares best so they only create information in one way. The result is the same people share it. Numbers stay high, maybe even grow slightly, but the business is reaching the same people over and over again and relevance doesn't spread. Interaction as an abstract measure isn't enough; you must consider the quality and range of people interacting.

Honesty and Transparency

In 2009, Marcus Sheridan was running a fibreglass pool company in Northern Virginia that was going out of business. It was the middle of the financial crisis in the United States. Nobody was buying pools.

So Sheridan, now known as the Sales Lion, did something crazy. He cut his $250,000 budget on conventional pay per click and radio ads and put all of his effort into producing free informational blog posts on his website. His goal? To answer every question anybody would ever have when it comes to fibreglass pools, even if it meant him telling a potential customer that his competition was a better option for her.

A perfect example is that his team wrote an article that outlines the problems with fibreglass pools. Talk about flipping the script? Why would anybody write an article on their own website that discusses the problems with the product that they sell? Another article that I found is called "Trilogy Casini vs. Greco Rectangular Fiberglass Pool Comparison." I don't know what those words mean, but for somebody in the middle-to-late stages of installing a pool this might be an important comparison to consider and is probably pretty hard to find information about.

Take a day and write down every question that you're asked about your product or service. If you have a team, ask them to do the same. Compile a master list of the questions and simply write the answers to each. Compile every answer into its own blog post or send it to a copywriter to formulate them into blog posts if you have the means, and publish them all.

Do this and not only will you become the most honest and transparent company in your industry, but you'll also become the resident experts because, by sharing your knowledge, knowledge that all companies who do what you do might have, you'll be seen as the expert.

Exclusion

Red Bull excludes most of the population in their marketing. They're extreme. Yet their energy drink flies off of the shelves even though it costs more than the competition.

If Red Bull tried to appeal to everybody they'd appeal to nobody. This is one of the secrets to their success. If you're into extreme sports you drink Red Bull.

Let's go back to your blog, err... I mean your movement. Why do you care about it? Is it because you're fed up with other real estate agents ripping off their clients?

Exclude the bad real estate agents from reading your posts. Include lines like, "if you don't care about your clients, click off this site right now and never come back." Commitment level to your site will increase because now your content stands for something.

You can bet proud real estate agents who are fed up with the dishonesty in their industry will jump at the opportunity to share your material.

Once someone hits your site they need to know four things within less than a second:

1. What it is.
2. Who the site is for.
3. How they will benefit.
4. Why they should care.

At the top of your site and all of your platforms you should have a mission statement of sorts. The Personal Trainer Development Center's is:

"The world's largest independent community of personal trainers. We're Dedicated to Improving the Perception of the Industry, and Your Success."

When somebody new hits your site and knows nothing about you, you've got very little time to "hook" them into wanting to learn more.

Consider the PTDC's statement above. Immediately upon reading the two sentences you know:

1. **What it is**: A community.
2. **Who it's for**: Personal trainers.
3. **How they will benefit**: It'll help them succeed.
4. **Why they should care**: Improve the perception of the industry.

Traction

A carpenter ant can be converted into a buyer, but you've usually got to generate traction out of them first.

Generating traction online is comprised of a series of "buy-ins" and with each one the user learns more about who you are and what you can do for them. A buy-in can be a number of things. For example,

- Reading a second article.
- Opting in to a social media network (liking your Facebook page, following you on Twitter/Linkedin Pinterest/Instagram, etc.).
- Opting in to your email list.
- Emailing you.
- Reading your about page.

Your job in designing your site and crafting your information is to provide your user with a logical next step – the second buy-in (reading the article that initially attracted them is the first) – that begins to generate traction with those that you want to serve.

Know where your user is coming from. If somebody hasn't heard of you yet and you get any kind of search engine traffic, then the second place that they'll go to after reading your article is your "about" page. The about page is not about you, it's about what you can do for your reader. It is also usually the highest trafficked page on your site of new users. That, and it should be your best lead generator.

Write your about page like a mini-sales letter.

1. **Benefit-rich** headline and lede.
2. **Value**
3. **Logic**
4. Multiple calls-to-action to additional sources of "buy-ins" to generate traction throughout (Facebook like, email opt-in, Twitter follow, etc.).

Have a headline that hooks a reader identifying the major benefit that you solve.

Follow with a lede – a few more sentences on the problem, or problems, and why they are important to your ideal customer.

Follow with a few things to do immediately to solve it. Link to some content if you like.

Follow with proof elements or logic: such as testimonials, awards, etc.

And, throughout the entire thing, include multiple places for the user to commit further to you by "liking" your Facebook page, joining your email list, or wherever else you've provided yourself an opportunity to continue following up.

Feel free to check out the PTDC's about page for an example at www.theptdc.com/about-us/

Viral Video

Videos share well. But is creating a viral video a sure-fire way to blow up a company or brand? I'm not convinced.

If you're a performer, then a viral video can make or break your career. What about other businesses? I was surprised at the instant drop-off in views on various YouTube channels that had been successful in hosting viral videos.

The pattern was always the same, 3,000-4,000 views on all of the videos leading up to the viral one consisting of at least 800,000 views. After the one success, however, views dropped back down to about 500 each.

This pattern tells me two things:

1. A small percentage of people actually check out the makers of the videos to see what they're all about. They watch 2-3 previous videos before clicking off.

2. Nobody cares about future projects if they're unrelated to the original video.

There are a few examples of videos that have launched successful companies. I'm not saying don't do it, but don't base your businesses success off of trying to go "viral." Instead, use video as a medium to appeal to your ideal viewer.

My suggestion is to look at video the same way you look at blog posts. Entertain first, but add in some education to show what your company or brand is about. Speak not just about your product, but about everything that your ideal consumer is interested in. The goal is to connect with your potential customer, not attract video carpenter ants.

Jack of All Trades

Choose one medium and make it your focus.

If you want to write, create videos that support your blog. If you decide to make videos, use the blog posts to support the video. If you podcast, then use your writing and video to support your podcast. Have one central gathering place and use all other types of media to feed into it.

Trying to do too many things at once early on causes too much dissipation. Later, once you've built up a platform, you can begin to work on multiple mediums at once. Focus on what you do best and what energizes you for now.

Focus

We were riding our bikes through the Santa Teresa National Park in Uruguay. Buzzing down a hill enjoying the wind on my face, something smacked my cheek. I stopped, and then I saw them.

Thousands of dragonflies; it was a beautiful sight. Cars whizzed by not noticing a thing. I would have whizzed by not noticing a thing. But when I stopped and focused it appeared – a whole world that would have passed me by.

When you stop and focus you see things that others don't.

That's how you get ahead.

Not by reading books. Not by consuming more information. And not by thinking that you need to do "one more thing" and everything will work out. It's by stopping to focus. To think.

Our need to focus hasn't changed. What has is the amount of distraction that we face.

The New Search

Feeds have become really good at reverse-engineering search. Everything from your age, gender, and location to your click signals (actions you take online) are tracked and a profile is being built about you. Advertisers use this, but so does everyone from Google to Facebook and Amazon.

So while you might still type in a keyword to search on any of the sites I listed above, the results that you get in response will be different to mine. They are specific to you. Not only that, but the sites that have an existing feed have become really good at showing you what you want to see before you even ask for it.

Earlier I spoke about the filter bubble phenomenon – we see what the system has predetermined that we want to see.

The Intangible Element

You need one thing.

An intangible element – it sets you apart.

This one thing doesn't have to be different or unique from your competition, although it could be, it just needs to be *your* thing.

The intangible element does two things:

1. It gives people a reason to talk about you rather than somebody else.

"This widget's great. It has an auto clean feature so I don't need to wash it by hand."

2. It helps a person justify a buying decision both to themselves and to others.

Buyer's remorse doesn't just happen after a purchase – the anticipation of it might stop the transaction from taking place. And buyer's remorse depends more on whether somebody feels like others will view him or her as stupid for purchasing, not just what they themselves think. An intangible element enables a buyer to feel like they can justify a purchase.

Find your intangible element. Here are a few examples of categories:

- Specific specs (especially with electronics).
- Qualifications / awards won by you or your company.
- A specific feature (doesn't have to be unique) of your product. A famous example is the Blendtec Blender being able to blend anything in their now-famous "Will It Blend" videos. This isn't unique to them, but they made it theirs.

What's your intangible element?

"ALWAYS REMEMBER THAT TRUSTING WHAT THEY'RE BUYING ISN'T CRAP AND THAT THEY AREN'T GETTING RIPPED OFF ARE MOST PEOPLE'S STRONGEST MOTIVATORS."

- @jon_ptdc

Perceived quality

The success, or failure, of a blog post, status update, or any other type of material that you produce online is dependent on a few factors, and one of them is perceived quality. Notice that I said 'perceived' and this has created some issues. Actual quality doesn't have as much of an impact as it should in terms of how much the message or content gets passed around.

A common piece of bad advice is to keep your writing short because short writing gets read more. This may be true, but it also gets shared less. I hate to say it, but the goal of your free front-facing material (blog post, social media status update, podcast, YouTube video, etc.) is that it works for you.

In other words, your front-facing content has a job to do. Its primary job is to find people, or appeal to existing people, by piquing their interest and acquiring their buy-in (for example: signing up to a mailing list to learn more or joining your Facebook community.)

It's when they opt-in to learn more that you hit them with your high-value materials. These materials are generally more thorough and don't need to follow many of the "rules" I outline in this book. In a sense, the point of any front-facing materials is to create the perception of expertise to enable you an opportunity to prove your expertise later. Flip the script and you'll have a hard time gaining traction. Not to say that it cannot be done but you will have a harder time.

There are three main ways to create a perception of quality on the front end. (Note: if you're already an influential expert then these things matter less because people generally already trust you and are willing to share your work):

1. **Length:** 1,800-3,500 words for a blog post seems to be the sweet spot. Still, don't be verbose for the sake of being verbose. Keep it as short as possible and as long as necessary. Just don't think that blog posts need to be short because peoples' attentions spans are short. Accept that most won't carefully read your blog post no matter how short you make it. Its job is to appeal, so that people become more interested and decide to invest the time to read your more premium materials or dedicate more time to investigating your company.

2. **Sources:** Back up your statements with research if possible and link to sources or others as much as possible. If you're making a claim and nobody knows who you are, the hope is that they will trust at least one of your sources enough to feel confident in passing along your material.

3. **Borrowing Legitimacy:** The most common way to do this is to quote other experts. You can also create legitimacy by giving your work titles. For example, I had a referral system that I described, and suggested that personal trainers follow. I called it the "referral ensure" system. The minute something has a name it seems like a thing. Even a name as terrible as "referral ensure" seemed to work.

I'm not saying that you shouldn't always strive to put out the best material possible. Far from it. Understanding the purpose for each type of content will help you make your work more effective.

The only real exceptions to this rule are sites that already have a large/dedicated audience. With an established critical mass of followers actual quality should definitely be the first and only priority.

Speaking of that, every piece of content that you publish fits into one of three categories ...

The Three Things Every Good Page / Blog Has

Successful content marketing, be it video, audio, or written, requires three distinct types of content. They are:

Viral: Anything that elicits an emotional response will share well. Jonah Berger, a professor at the Wharton School of Business and author of *Contagious: Why Things Catch On*, has shown that activating emotion and physiological arousal leads to a significant bump in virality. Both happiness and anger are good. Also consider IIIAF. If you can make somebody happy and give her a tool to project to her audience that she appears intelligent, intellectual, interesting, attractive, and/or funny then the chances that you'll get an increase in your vanity metrics such as "likes" and page views will improve. This isn't to say that you'll go viral every time but there are certainly guidelines to follow.

Often times the right answer is one that takes the middle ground. If you already have a strong audience then you can go viral right up until the final node on your existing network by viewing a topic from all angles. Just don't expect it to share well beyond people who haven't yet heard about you. With all of this having been said, you don't necessarily want to go viral most of the time anyway.

Value-Add Posts: These are posts that are meant to give value to your existing followers but will not spread virally. Don't expect them to increase your numbers, but they add sensational value to your existing audience and help to establish you as the go-to for your subject.

Calls To Action: This is where you try and get a follower to join an email list or buy a product. For front-facing content this is usually an "ask" to get somebody to join an email list or enter in his information so that you can follow up. A specific call to purchase something may also work if it's a low-priced offer.

There is no one best ratio of these three types of content. That, and it will change as your audience grows. At the beginning, for example, value-add posts aren't as important for no other reason than you have nobody to add value to. As such, your ratio should be closer to 80 : 10 : 10 viral : value : action.

But then take someone in my position with the Personal Trainer Development Center. The site already has a large audience with a strong community. Additionally, I've put pieces in place to gain new readers that work for me every day (my books, guest appearances all over the net, paid ads, and a huge archive of content that shows in various searches or gets passed along). As such, my priority with the front-facing blog has shifted. I no longer work to get new viewers for two reasons:

1. It happens organically and,
2. I already have more readers and potential customers than I'll ever need in many lifetimes.

My priority is not to get more people, it's to convert my existing readers into higher-levels of readiness to buy a product of mine if it solves one of their problems. As such, the ratio of content that I produce is closer to 10 : 70 : 20 viral : value : action.

The New York Times

One of the most fascinating developments in recent times has been the emergence of the blog. What started as an obscure information source used primarily by early adopters has now become the most widespread and powerful source of information.

Some argue that blogs have killed the newspaper. I don't agree. Blogs have forced the newspapers to evolve, and the New York Times is a perfect example.

The newspaper has been continuously published since 1851 under its current name and has won an astounding 114 Pulitzer Prizes. Throughout modern history it's been one of the most trusted sources of information in the world.

It's interesting that the most popular content on the website is almost entirely the blogs. In fact, at the time of writing this book, a tab on the front page on nytimes.com includes the three headings: Most E-Mailed, Most Viewed, and Recommended for You and a link to the opinion pages. If it's clear to the newspapers what type of material readers prefer, why are most companies still printing boring, factual articles?

Heck, the New York Times even subscribes to Google Ads. Now I can get a ripped six-pack while reading an editorial on the Republicans' position for the upcoming election.

As Ryan Holiday points out in his book, *Trust Me, I'm Lying: Confessions of a Media Manipulator*, ads are what pay the bills and page views are what drive ad revenue.

It's an archaic and inherently broken model that self-selects for sensationalistic writing, polarizing "link-baiting articles", and breaking, poorly-researched, news. It's no longer about producing the best content, or substantive writing, something that the NY Times has become known for; it's about producing the type of content that will get a lot of views.

Blogs started as a place where outsiders could ramble on about obscure points (funny enough, Jorn Barger, largely credited with creating the term weblog hated the sound of "blog." He capitalized the word in two places, WebLog, because, in his words, "the syllable 'blog' seemed so hideous.") Nowadays, blogs are the primary source of information passage in the world. Most modern companies have accepted their need for a blog but don't know where to start.

Blogs are personal. Readers must relate and connect to the content. They must care. And blogs can't survive based off of page views – because when they do, quality goes down and everybody loses.

The model for making money from a blog and/or news source must evolve. Front-facing material on a website is a place to gather people who believe in what you believe in and entice them to invest in a premium offering. As pay-per-click money continues to go down, you need to build out a source of information that people care about, and this all comes down to what they feel it says about them.

Your Morning Oatmeal

There comes a time in every man's life when he stops measuring his oatmeal.

A time when he realizes that a little more water or a few less oats won't make much of a difference.

What matters is that the oatmeal is made every morning, rain or shine.

Stop worrying whether or not what you're doing is the best way. There might be a best, and there might not. What really matters is that you keep on showing up.

Is this Über-Rational Secret Society Killing Creativity?

Mass rationality is an onslaught that is being brought forth by an evil group gaining power called the Arithmocracy (named by Anthony Tasgal in his award winning paper called "The Science of the Brands: Alchemy, Advertising and Accountancy").

According to Rory Sutherland, the arithomocracy is "a powerful left-brained administrative caste which attaches importance only to things which can be expressed in numerical terms or on a chart."

The accessibility of information and analytics allows companies to predict, measure, and strategize better than ever before but it's doing more harm than good. Vanity metrics are omnipresent and they take up valuable mental capacity, time, and money to spend, track, and attempt to improve. Some examples are Facebook 'likes," website views, and total free downloads.

According to New York Times Bestselling author Eric Ries, "the only metrics that entrepreneurs should invest energy in collecting are those that help them make decisions."

Keep it simple. Choose one or two actionable metrics and base your success off of them. Two examples might be: active users and, of course, sales. If your company has the resources to measure more and you feel like sales funnel metrics and A/B split-testing of certain pages or features of pages are important, then they could prove useful but you've got to have a lot of traffic to guarantee reliable results.

If you're just starting out though, then your job is to produce great work, not get caught up in measuring. Don't let the arithmocracy get to you. We've lost too many already to the cult of rationality.

The Age of Infotainment

Websites that contain high quality information are dying. For a site to succeed, it needs to master the art of infotainment and establish what the right balance is. Always strive to provide the best content that you can, but know what the goal of your different types of content is. I spoke earlier about the three types of content that every site has: value, viral, and call to action.

High quality information usually stays dormant unless strong influencers share the material. Even then, unless it truly is something special, it's not read thoroughly on the Internet. When trying to get material to spread the perception of quality is unfortunately more important than actual quality. This explains to a large extent why long-form posts with lots of references do in fact share better.

Maybe your split should be 80% entertainment and 20% information, or 60/40. Whatever it is, show your personality.

Pressing the share button has become a way to show off to the world what you want others to think of you. This means that profound information doesn't share well. Nobody wants to show off that they're ignorant towards a subject unless that subject is truly spectacular.

SEO Content

What's a more engaging title? "Tax help: a blog about how to get help with tax" or "How Jeff saved himself from a tax crisis and how you can too in 3 easy steps"?

I'd read the second article. Problem is SEO (search engine optimization) pundits will tell you to write the first because it ranks better in Google.

I know one thing about Google's algorithm. They currently have a room filled with the most brilliant people on the planet figuring out how to enable good information to flourish. Their goal is to punish spammers and marketers with poor information. And you know what?

They're going to succeed.

Remember when you used to see Answers.com or Yahoo answers show up first in every Google search you did? When was the last time you saw either of these sites?

Google is optimizing for high quality content and lots of interaction. This is perfect if you're passionate about your subject. The best part is that they're making it harder and harder to cheat. If you want your message to get out it must be commented on, shared, and read by real people –

not bots and not outsourcing companies in India that will "like" your post 40 times for $20/month (yes, this stuff exists and it's more prevalent than you think).

Moving forward SEO tricks will be less important. What will matter is that you get your meta-tags and titles on your sites (any SEO expert will be able to help you with this).

Add to this the obvious fact that you're writing content for your readers. The goal is to get them to share it with their trusted network. They're not going to share your spam, and the only people who will find it are the carpenter ants in the information gathering stage. To win, you've got to stay in the feed long enough so that when people are ready to buy you're the first person that they think of.

Post Less and Promote More

If you're new, there's no point in publishing a ton of value-laden material because no one will see it. Revisit your ratio of value : viral : action I've discussed a few times in this book. When you're starting out, post less and promote more.

Spend your time writing 1-3 really good posts each month and promote the heck out of them. Find groups related to your niche and network, attend events, reach out to other bloggers and add value, do anything you can to get an audience back to your site. Once you have a good readership, you can choose whether or not to post more often.

Another great strategy is to create content for a specific niche. Instead of writing an article on fat loss, write an article on fat loss for lawyers. Then promote it by seeking out all of the groups already developed that serve lawyers and send them the article to share with their audience. It takes some legwork, and lots of people will ignore you and say no when you ask them to share your material. But some will say yes, and that makes it all worth it.

Inherent Value

Packaging largely determines value. We have pre-existing notions of what is worth money and how much. And it has much less to do with logic than you may think.

If you want a newspaper and you walk into a store, you wouldn't think twice about paying a few dollars for the current issue. Yet when a news outlet asks for a few dollars a month for a subscription that not only provides digital access to each current issue, but also to the entire archive, the response is to click away and sometimes even cry foul.

Blog posts don't have much value. Attempting to get people to register for a monthly membership and hiding your best material behind a paywall will limit your growth. The value of your site and network has much more to do with how big and dedicated you can grow it versus how much money you can make from it today. Instead of hiding your best stuff behind a paywall and then creating even more material to appeal to people who will hopefully pay you to see it, publish your best stuff. Let it work for you to bring in readers.

The key to content marketing is to become a master at repurposing content. Here's a number of different options to package the material from your best blog posts into products for sale that people are willing to pay for (vs. blog posts that people aren't willing to pay for):

1. Hire an editor to take your best blog posts and assemble them into a book (you will probably have to fill in some blanks). Create a Kindle and audio version of the book as well.

2. Choose 1-3 different topics that you write about a lot and create an audio course with more detail than what is in your blog posts.

3. Choose the one topic that you know best and create a full video course going into a lot of detail on it.

4. Host digital webinar events where people pay a fee to log on for you to teach them.

5. Record these webinars and sell the recording either as a one-off or as a box set.

6. Schedule live events.

7. Develop a high-level coaching program walking people through the action steps in your blog posts.

Action!

Nick Tumminello is a top strength coach who has built a killer reputation on the Internet. So much so that he sold his business in Baltimore and moved to Florida to focus on developing his Internet presence. He still trains select clients but has released a few successful books, travels the globe speaking, and creates DVDs and digital books sold via the Internet. He does this all from his beachside apartment.

Nick's got one rule and I'm proud to say that, after speaking with him, I've adopted his rule:

Every post must have at least one actionable step that the reader can immediately take to solve the problem from the post.

Here's a simple example:

"Water does so much more than simply hydrate you. It boosts energy, revs the metabolism, and nourishes the skin. For most 8 glasses of water a day is enough, which comes to about 1.9 litres.

Here's an easy way to keep track of your water intake: Carry a 500ml bottle with you with 4 elastic bands wrapped around. After you finish a bottle, take off a band and refill the bottle. At the end of the day you should have removed all 4 bands."

Novel idea isn't it? Problem + solution = post. Makes sense to me.

Who Are You Writing For?

Are you writing what you want to write or what you think you should write?

The Dreaded Blank Piece of Paper

There's nothing more intimidating than a blank page. Writing high quality blog posts is hard. Here's a great template for writing a quality article (or even a great status update):

1. Tell a story (make it personal).

2. Highlight the problem from the story.

3. Restate the problem in more general terms.

4. Outline the steps to a solution.

5. Conclusion.

A couple notes here:

First off, the conclusion is not a simple wrap-up of the article. That's a copout. Leave the reader with some food for thought. A motivational phrase works well, as does wrapping up the story from step 1.

Next, try to pick out obscure references in your story for your reader to connect with. If you're speaking about a fat loss workout, joke about an infomercial from years back, like Jane Fonda. It'll give the reader something to laugh about and also open up the opportunity to end the post by relating back to the Jane Fonda workout. With every status update and blog post try to have one 'sticky' point or reference that jumps out of the page, or screen.

Instead of staring at a blank piece of paper write down my five steps on a pad of paper. Use point form to fill them in. Then, as you write, simply fill in the blanks. Bingo, bango, bongo – blog post!

But what if you hate writing? I made the point earlier to choose one medium and make it your focus. Don't think that you have to have a blog. You could have a podcast, or YouTube show, or something else. Or maybe you'd do best as a curator of work where your website simply becomes an archive of cool and interesting things you come across. Maria Popova with brainpickings.org is a great example of a curator that's now one of the most influential figures online.

"ART MAKES THE SNOOZE BUTTON OBSOLETE."

- @jon_ptdc

As Short as Possible, and as Long as Necessary

I know I said earlier that lengthy posts convey value and get passed around more. This is true, but it's not a good enough reason to become purposefully verbose.

This book is just over 23,000 words long because that's how long it needed to be.

Less is not more when it comes to blogs and status updates. Just enough is more. Get in, get dirty, make your point, and get out.

You have one rule:

As short as possible, and as long as necessary.

Bullets and Lists

Italian philosopher Umberto Eco once said "the list doesn't destroy culture; it creates it. Wherever you look in cultural history, you will find lists." In *The Infinity of Lists: An Illustrated Essay* he goes on to say, "the list is the origin of culture. It's part of the history of art and literature. What does culture want? To make infinity comprehensible. It also wants to create order."

There simply is no better way to organize information. Yet so many are quick to call lists a lower type of communication. This could not be further from the truth.

I'll be the first to say that the type of people who read lists called "50 things that all successful people do" are clearly missing the point because successful people don't read lists about what successful people do. But when it comes to organizing the onslaught of amazing, diverse, and brilliant knowledge that you have in your brain, bullet point lists, either on their own or contained in a status update or blog post are effective. It allows people to quickly find what they are looking for.

You'll notice that I use a lot of lists in this book. Short lists.

Romania

Years ago I had the Personal Trainer Development Center website audited by an outside party. I was about to undergo a major redesign and needed an un-biased analysis of the site. There was one major surprise.

Romania was the site's third best source of traffic.

I expected the United States and Canada to be 1 and 2, but Romania beat out all the European countries, and the fitness-crazed Australia. When I looked into it the reason became clear.

The reason was Livia Vaduva.

One day I noticed her "like" a post and thought nothing of it. The next day there was another, and another, and another. Soon she started commenting on posts. This went on for weeks. The minute I posted anything I knew to expect a comment from her and I also responded. One day Livia sent me a long email.

I was inundated with emails and didn't want to read her life story. I'm happy I did. I was moved by what this amazing woman had gone through to become fit, and I stayed awake until 2 a.m. composing a response. Since then we've built up a great relationship.

When I told her about the stunning results of my site audit she wasn't surprised. It turned out she'd been posting every single article I publish onto the biggest Romanian workout group on the net. Talk about scaling!

The same people will comment and "like" your material. Your first inclination is to get frustrated. Don't. These are your most important followers whether you know them personally or not.

The push right now is to hire personal assistants to handle mundane tasks like answering emails and responding to basic inquires. This is fine, but have personal communication forwarded. When you have a successful article or product launch you'll be overwhelmed with emails. Stay awake for three days straight if you need to. Answer them all with the best damn answers you can muster up.

This is what you've been working for. People are interested in you. They've come to you for help. For advice. For guidance. Stay home from work that day. Cancel your plans. Go to Starbucks and annoy the barista by ordering a medium and look confused when she asks you if you really wanted a grandé and insist upon a medium, but answer every single message. The iron is hot. Strike it before it cools off.

Automate and outsource other aspects of your life. Hire a personal chef and pay somebody to clean your house if you have to. Never automate your personal interaction. Your response may just get you posted on the largest workout forum in Romania.

Who Shares?

Ben Bruno used to be the centre of information in the fitness world. He published two lists weekly. One was of the top blog posts and the other consisted of the top videos from the fitness industry.

Ben held a lot of power. He dictated what got read and what didn't. Most bloggers tried to get on his list. They were going about it all wrong.

They should have cared about the people already on the list.

Every week I would go through the list and email bloggers I didn't know. I'd send them all a personal message saying that I enjoyed their material on "X" topic. My aim is always to build a relationship with them, but they aren't my targets.

I wanted to gain access to their feed. In building a relationship with them I'd gain access to their feeds, whatever network(s) they were on. When I did I watched it like a hawk.

You should be looking to identify the people interacting with these bloggers. These are your targets. These are the Greg O'Hare's who will spread your word.

The pattern will look something like this: There will be 2-3 key people commenting and "liking" that seem to share every piece of content by the blogger. The same names will keep popping up on a number of different bloggers' walls.

After recognizing this pattern, it became obvious to me that these people were building the paths to connect the fitness world with information. I needed to make them all fans of my work so they would share every piece of content / publish.

Slowly but surely I made connections with all of the road builders through comment threads, personal messages, or by reaching out to them on their own networks. Once they interacted with me on one of my posts I sent a private message thanking them for their support. This was all it took.

My wall became a flurry of activity. The status updates that I published shot to the top of the feed for a huge variety of people from fitness professionals to workout fanatics. The trick was not finding the influencers; it was finding the people who share the influencer's work.

Oh, and One More Thing...

...You should be the one publishing the list.

People Buy People, Not Products, Not Companies, and Not "Brands"

Anybody who reads your blog cares about you, not your product. The purpose of a blog is to show your human side even if you're a multinational corporation.

Write in the first person. Use *I* and *me* instead of *you* or *your*. People connect with humans, not robots who write generic information. They want to share information that resonates with them. Show your smiling face.

Would you read and share something that's written by a large impersonal corporation that's given you no reason to trust it or would you prefer to hear from Sarah at General Electric?

Nobody knows who Sarah is or even if she is a real person, but you're immediately drawn into listening to her. Sarah makes the experience more real. You can connect to Sarah. You look forward to hearing from Sarah.

The Time to be Humble has Passed

You're the product. People will be willing to pay a premium for people, and the products and services that they represent. A buying decision is more often based upon the security that what the person is buying a) won't suck and b) won't make them feel like they look stupid for buying it. In following a person and building up trust with them online, a prospect feels more at ease deciding to buy.

Your front line is everything and your social media accounts and blogs are your front line.

People have chosen to engage with your material - you didn't force them. You're the expert. Your company is the best option - there is no second-guessing.

Don't ever write "in my opinion." We know it's your opinion.

You're the one writing it. Be confident.

A blog post with three tax tips isn't special. Any accountant can write that. A blog post about how you saved a client thousands of dollars is effective. Better yet, add a picture of the postcard they sent you from the vacation they can now afford. *I'd hire you.*

Show off. Speak about your past and why it's helped you develop your ideas. Show that you're human by talking about your struggles and how you overcame them. Build rapport with your audience by asking for help in areas outside of your expertise. Talk specifically about the people you've helped.

Be specific and paint a picture.

Why would anybody hire you if you don't believe in yourself?

"THE BABE RUTH RULE: NOBODY REMEMBERS HOW MANY TIMES YOU STRIKE OUT. THEY ONLY REMEMBER THE DINGERS."

- @jon_ptdc

I Want In

If you're in a position of power people will share your post in an attempt to climb the Internet social ladder. It's a way of becoming part of a club and can be a powerful source of traffic for popular bloggers. If you already have a big following, go out of your way to profile active members of your community.

If you don't yet have a big following but want to take advantage of this you have to project success.

Here are some tricks to make you appear bigger and more important than you are so that others will build you up. It's not deceitful and you don't need to lie. These are simply ways to make note of particular things happening.

1. **Answer questions sent in by readers**. Whenever you get a question, answer it publicly on your blog or social media outlet (or both) and be sure to mention that a reader sent in the question.

2. **Reach out to well-known bloggers.** Ask permission to repost their old material giving them sole credit as the author and a link back to their site. Most industry experts have years' worth of old material that collects dust. They're ecstatic when somebody wants to republish it. When the post is live, send them a message with the link saying thank you. They might just share it, passing on some of their credibility to you. This is largely how I built up my platform in the early stages.

Being the expert is a position of power. Once you're there people will rush to join you. Be creative if you're having trouble moving up the ranks. Just make sure your content matches your status or you won't stay at the top for very long.

Call to Action

Do you want your reader to buy your product after reading your blog post? Maybe you want them to enter your sales funnel by "liking" your Facebook page or signing up for your mailing list.

Always include a call to action. Ask your reader to like your page or enter their email for more information.

How else are they supposed to know?

Giving it Away for Free

When the PTDC released its free e-book entitled *101 Personal Trainer Mistakes*, it resulted in the biggest spike we'd ever seen. The site received 12,000 visits the first day and we were able to capture 1,600 email addresses in the first week.

When was the last time your company got 1,600 leads from dedicated consumers in a week?

The book cost $5 to produce and took much less time to put together than you may think. I opened a Google spreadsheet and asked my network of top fitness professionals to send in any mistakes they've made on the job. Two weeks later I had a list of 120 mistakes. I sent the list out and asked people to write in solutions.

All I did was compile it into a word document and convert the whole thing to .pdf. Instead of trying to come up with everything myself I put aside my ego and asked for help allowing others to contribute. The result was a better product than anything I could have hoped to produce. I could have sold the book. It's got tremendous value for any personal trainer looking to improve.

Instead I gave it away for free. The result was that it went purposefully viral. The PTDC had passed 1,000 views a day twice before the book was released. It's never been below 1,000 views since and now reaches many millions a year. That book is largely responsible for the site's success. The massive shareability of the Ebook created the base my site needed.

Most companies don't show appreciation to their customers. You're different. Show your customers they matter. Give them gifts.

Deeper Down the Rabbit Hole

Want to really get down to details? Try to predict the state of awareness of a reader consuming your status update (this doesn't apply as much to blog posts as your goal is to make those more evergreen or always relevant).

Here's a sample overview:

- Monday is the start of the week. Get it started right. Motivation and quick tips work well. People don't have much time Monday but a quick pick-me-up is good.

- Friday culminates a week of hard work. So wrap up. Lists work well.

- Wednesday is work. People are generally busy on Wednesdays so it's not a great day to publish. If you do, content based on overcoming boundaries, sticking with it, or overcoming adversity work well.

- Tuesdays and Thursdays are great days for more informative posts.

- Publish and market articles early in the morning. Breakfast time is a big window. Morning is a great time for information-rich posts or shares of quality information as people are getting a start on their productive day.

- Night-time is for entertainment. Infotainment posts work well when published at night. Wait until after dinnertime. I've found 7:30-9pm to be the best time for posting but it does change and is specific to your audience.

- Sunday morning is the best time to get people to read. This is when you publish your weekly recaps of the best articles and videos in your industry.

For every audience it's different. There are two considerations when deciding the best time to post a status update:

1. **When your audience has nothing to do.** For most this is first thing in the morning, lunchtime, and at night. For office workers, later on in the work day on Thursdays and Fridays is also good because that's when people procrastinate.

2. **When your audience is physiologically aroused.** In a study performed by Jonah Berger, physiological arousal increased sharing from 33%-75%. If you can figure out when your audience goes to the gym or even a walk, share your viral materials right afterwards.

Based on these guidelines, create a posting schedule. I've produced a free one at **www.viralnomics.com/status-update/** that you can grab and fill out. My suggestion is to fill out your status updates in bulk in advance. My team generally schedules them in twice a week, on Sunday and Wednesday.

Intrigue

Want to get somebody to click on your link? Ask a question. Intrigue will help you stand out from the noise.

Feeds move quickly. You need to do something that grabs somebody's attention and makes him or her want to click. You could have the best material in the World, but if nobody clicks on your link (usually dependent on your title and picture) then it won't get read and people will go back to sharing pictures of cats.

There are a couple techniques that seem to work well to get a person's attention. Many of them stem from intrigue.

1. **Ask a question.** Usually it's a question that your reader already knows the answer to. The intrigue stems from wanting to make sure that they aren't missing anything and the later share stems from showing off that they know the answer.

Consider the differences between these two titles:

The Most Stable Shape in the World is a Triangle

Or

Is the Triangle the Most Stable Shape in the World?

2. **Include a "bit that you can't miss."** In the headline include an element that makes people feel like they need to figure it out or can't miss one part.

Consider the differences between these two titles:

8 Things You Need to Know About Using Fluffy Cushions

Or

8 Things (#3 surprised even me) You Need to Know About Using Fluffy Cushions

You'd be pretty hard pressed to find someone who wouldn't want to know what #3 is.

Make Your Content Easy to Share

If you work in a tight-knit neighbourhood there's no excuse for your material not to share.

The goal isn't to appeal to everybody with every post. The goal is to write a post that hits home for a small percentage of your customers.

A plumbing blog should speak about one specific issue having to do with toilet maintenance one week and the difference between clay and PVC pipes the next. You'll attract the one or two people who are dealing with the specific issue and they'll call you for a job.

Also, people talk. Imagine how powerful it is if I write a post about low back pain and how to treat it. I speak specifically about a client I helped. I'm willing to bet that somebody reading my post knows someone who suffers from low back pain. They send my material on, and I have a quality lead.

Appealing to the masses is fine if you have lofty goals. For a neighbourhood company, though, blogs need to be personal and specific. Their aim is to appeal to a small minority of the neighbourhood.

How many customers do you really need for a neighbourhood business? There are 3 ways to make more money:

1. Get more customers
2. Charge more per transaction
3. Generate more transactions per customer

Businesses put a lot of focus on getting more customers, but #2 and #3 above increase revenues just as much. Wouldn't you love to have a dedicated recurring clientele?

Why Most Companies Will Fail

Much of this information is not proven and never will be. The social media landscape changes too fast. The feed will change before anybody can figure out what the ROI (Return On Investment) of a retweet or Facebook "like" is. It's impossible to print materials to train people appropriately to use the specifics of a social media platform. What doesn't change is the psychology behind it and that's why this book is focused mostly on theory backed by research. You must take the initiative to adapt the theory to your situation.

In big business it's easiest to follow the status quo. If you screw up trying something new, it's your butt on the line. If you work the way your company has always worked and it gets your company adequate results you keep your job.

One TV ad costs tens of thousands of dollars. Its intent is to appeal to a potential consumer's subconscious. I'm not even convinced that this was a good use of money years ago, but it's definitely not now in the generation of PVRs.

Why not reach out to people who have already become engaged in a community surrounding your product or service and gain their trust and support? They're out there – you just need to find them.

If you can't find a community, then you're in luck. You get to be first. Build it yourself. I promise there are a lot of people who care deeply about what you do and want a voice.

Stop doing the same thing as everybody else because they've all been doing it for years. Times have changed. Most won't adapt. If you do you'll blow past the competition and never look back. I challenge you to take the risk.

Stop Trying to Appeal to Customers

Future customers don't care about you now. They aren't looking for your information, and if they do happen to see it, they won't stop to take a look.

Appeal to people passionate about the same ideas and ideals as you by articulating their thoughts and desires. That way, they help you stay in the feed long enough for others to find you when they – or somebody that they know – need your product or service.

What's the idea or message that your company represents? Why do you get out of bed in the morning? What drives you?

The majority of people don't create – they share. And the primary reason why people share your information and your name is to show off what they already do or know.

You're giving them a tool to project their own thoughts when they're not comfortable, don't have the ability, or lack the time to do it themselves.

People gain perceived social equity (get a hit of IIIAF) when they can prove that somebody else justifies their thinking. Allow others to publicly justify their own thoughts and passions through your material.

Social media accounts have become an extension of oneself. Be the creator — this is your goal.

What's Your Legacy?

Are you in this for the long term?

Cheap products are sold on fear and emotion with pressure sales and closing techniques. Companies providing poor service and low quality goods must focus on shoving a product in as many people's faces as possible with the hope that a small percentage buy.

These companies don't last. No one tells friends about them and word about their product won't spread. The products collect dust before showing up on Craigslist or on the buyer's lawn years later. If you write a book for the money and it doesn't sell, you're left with nothing. Or, in the words of author Neil Gaiman, "if you didn't get the money then you didn't have anything. If I did the work I was proud of and I didn't get the money, at least I'd have the work."

Your product is good. Your service is the best. You deserve a legacy.

Foster relationships and give your customers a reason to share. Help them succeed and you'll rise up to the top with them. Give your followers a reason to boast. Make them care about you and they'll spread the word.

They'll create your legacy for you.

It All Comes Down to You

To become the expert you must become the voice of those who don't have the confidence, time, or drive to develop their own. You need to change your focus and begin to appeal to the converted. It's time to become comfortable articulating the quiescent needs, urges, desires, and beliefs of your target audience.

I've introduced you to the cast, showed you that what's new is really old, and put the pieces in place for you to rise to power within your own network. Now it's up to you to decide the next steps. So what do you say, will you be "the guy"?

"ON YOUR JOURNEY THERE WILL BE RESISTANCE. YOU MAY OUTGROW FRIENDS. YOUR FAMILY MAY THINK THAT YOU'RE CUCKOO—THIS IS FINE. THIS IS GOOD."

- @jon_ptdc

Index

'TILL NEXT TIME!

- JON

Made in the USA
Lexington, KY
12 February 2017